D1761014

Humanist Marxism and Wittgensteinian social philosophy

Susan M. Easton

Humanist Marxism and Wittgensteinian social philosophy

Manchester University Press

Published by
MANCHESTER UNIVERSITY PRESS
Oxford Road, Manchester M13 9PL, UK
and
51 Washington Street, Dover
New Hampshire 03820, USA

British Library cataloguing in publication data
Easton, Susan M.
Humanist Marixsm and Wittgensteinian social philosophy.
1. Marx, Karl – Sociology 2. Wittgenstein, Ludwig – Sociology
3. Social sciences – Philosophy
I. Title
300'.1 B3305.M74
ISBN 0-7190-0935-9

Library of Congress cataloging in publication data
Easton, Susan M.
Humanist Marxism and Wittgensteinian social philosophy.
Includes bibiliographical references and index.
1. Marx, Karl, 1818–1883. 2. Wittgenstein, Ludwig, 1889-1951. I. Title.
B3305.M74E27 1983 335,4'112 83-9391
ISBN 0-7190-0935-9

Printed in Great Britain
by Redwood Burn Ltd, Trowbridge, Wiltshire

For Frances, Michael and Charlotte

Contents

Acknowledgements

I would like to thank the publishers of *Studies in Soviet Thought* for permission to include a revised version of an article 'Facts, values and Marxism' which appeared in the August 1977 edition (XVII, 2, pp. 117–34, copyright © 1977 D. Reidel Publishing Company, Dordrecht, Holland) and the editors of *Social Praxis* for permission to use a revised version of an article 'Conventionalism and the limits to social change' which originally appeared in the 1978 issue (V 3–4, pp. 323–41, copyright © 1978 Mouton Publishers, The Hague, The Netherlands). I would also like to express thanks to colleagues who commented on earlier drafts of the manuscript.

The weapon of criticism cannot, of course, replace criticism by weapons, material force must be overthrown by material force; but theory also becomes a material force as soon as it has gripped the masses.

Marx

What is the use of studying philosophy if all that it does for you is to enable you to talk with some plausibility about some abstruse questions of logic, etc., & if it does not improve your thinking about the important questions of everyday life,

Wittgenstein

Introduction

An elucidation and defence of the central tenets of humanist Marxism is offered here via an examination of Wittgenstein's key ideas. At first sight the links between the two approaches might seem tenuous given that little effort has been made to show the social relevance of Wittgenstein's ideas despite the much-acclaimed philosophical revolution brought about by his work. Instead Wittgenstein has become a pillar of the philosophical establishment, respected for his philosophical purity, whereas Marx, who tried to show the relevance of philosophy to political life has been derided by professional philosophers for this reason.[1] The strong commitment to the separation of philosophy from practice in Anglo-Saxon philosophy is reflected in the fondness of Wittgenstein's disciples for logical puzzle-solving and the superficial features of linguistic usage. It is perhaps not surprising that, with few exceptions, philosophers and social scientists have failed to see the fundamental similarities between the ideas of Marx and Wittgenstein. Indeed Marxism has been seen as alien to Anglo-Saxon philosophy while Wittgenstein has been identified with this tradition. 'One of the greatest misfortunes that can affect a writer of great intellectual seriousness and strong ethical passions', as Janik and Toulmin have argued, 'is to have his ideas "naturalized" by the English'.[2] Comparing Shaw and Wittgenstein, they observe that:

> All the moral indignation, political barbs and social vitriol of George Bernard Shaw were robbed of their power the moment the English public for which he wrote pigeonholed him securely as an Irish wag and a comic playwright. And something of the same fate has shaped the current reputation of Ludwig Wittgenstein – at any rate, as he is seen by most professional English-speaking philosophers in Britain and America.[3]

Wittgenstein may have lent encouragement to this Anglicisation of his thought, thereby obscuring his links with his German philosophical heritage, by claiming to have little knowledge of the history of philosophy as if he developed his ideas in a vacuum, arriving on the scene like Athena out of the head of Zeus. In fact he refers to numerous other philosophers, including Plato, Augustine, Kant, Schopenhauer and Kierkegaard, in his work. He was also immersed in the cultural and artistic debates of pre-war Austria. His remark should therefore be taken either as a jest or as an over-statement of his philosophical independence. Furthermore, in *Culture and Value*, Wittgenstein acknowledged that he was part of the intellectual drift of his time rather than a solitary genius:

> I think there is some truth in my idea that I really only think reproductively. I don't believe I have ever *invented* a line of thinking. I have always taken one over from someone else. I have simply straightaway seized on it with enthusiasm for my work of clarification. That is how Boltzmann, Hertz, Schopenhauer, Frege, Russell, Kraus, Loos, Weininger, Spengler, Sraffa have influenced me ....[4]

Wittgenstein's links with Cambridge have tended to overshadow his connections with German thought, even though during the period from 1908 to 1937 he spent less than eight years in England, of which three were spent studying engineering at the University of Manchester.[5] Through his association with Russell and Moore, Wittgenstein has been identified with the English empiricists. Yet many of his ideas, such as the need for a general critique of language expressed in the *Tractatus*, had reached maturity before his contact with Cambridge and had their origins in the post-Kantian tradition dominating the pre-war Viennese cultural milieu.[6] The later writings also bear the imprint of these Austrian influences: his abandonment of the representational view of language for a functional analysis in the *Investigations* reflects the move away from ornamentation to functionality in architecture, as well as the more direct influence of discussions with the economist Piero Sraffa.[7] In place of a general representational theory, Wittgenstein focused on the use of language within a plurality of contexts and in doing so revealed an affinity with Marx. This is reflected in their approach to epistemological and philosophical problems which militates against the erection of fixed dichotomies and antinomies, the endless classification, polarisation and fragmentation characteristic of much Anglo-Saxon philosophy and instead appeals to the practice of everyday life to solve philosophical problems. As Marx says:

> We see how subjectivity and objectivity, spirituality and materiality, activity and suffering, lose their antithetical character, and thus their existence as such antitheses only within the framework of society: we see how the resolution of the *theoretical* antitheses is *only* possible in a *practical* way by virtue of the practical energy of man. Their resolution is therefore by no means merely a problem of understanding, but a *real* problem of life, which *philosophy* could not solve precisely because it conceived this problem as *merely* a theoretical one.[8]

In a more jocular vein he writes:

> Kant and Fichte soar to heavens blue
>   Seeking for some distant land,
> I but seek to grasp profound and true
>   That which in the street I find.[9]

But whilst it will be argued that Marx's remarks on ideology presuppose an epistemology which is radically different from that of Anglo-Saxon philosophy, this is not wholly explicit in his writings. It is only in the work of later humanist Marxists such as Lukács and Goldmann that this epistemology is more fully articulated.[10] As Marxism embraces a set of ideas which are constantly changing rather than fixed dogmas enshrined in textbooks, we will consider the way in which contemporary Marxism, as well as Marx himself, has sought to deal with philosophical and methodological problems. However, there are certain strands within Marxism which emphasise Marx's rejection of humanism in favour of scientism and which are in danger of reverting to an Anglicised conception of philosophy far removed from practice.[11] While Marx's work provides evidence for both interpretations, it will be argued, however, that a humanistic approach, drawing heavily from Hegel's ideas, provides a more fruitful source of concepts for the analysis of modern society. But to reject empirical realism and to demonstrate Marx's debt to Hegel is not to reduce Marxism to idealism. Neither Marx nor Hegel can be seen as idealist, for each seeks to transcend the distinction between materialism and idealism.

Chapter I investigates the epistemological assumptions underpinning Marx's account of ideology, employing Wittgensteinian concepts to contrast it with its empirical realist counterpart. Chapter II constitutes a critical examination of the essence–appearance distinction in Marx's later theory of knowledge and the work of more recent theorists. Chapter III considers how Marxists and Wittgensteinian social philosophers transcend the fact–value distinction, rejecting both extremes of scientism and moralism. In Chapter IV it is argued that the Marxian–Wittgensteinian notion of a world-view is the most appropriate notion for understanding the relationship between ideas and social life. The following two chapters consider the problems of conventionalism and relativism arising from the notion of a world-view and indicate a possible solution, using the notions of universality and practice. The remaining chapters deal with possible objections to a reconciliation between humanist Marxism and Wittgensteinian social philosophy: Chapter VII attempts to distance Marx from Wittgenstein on the basis of the materialism of the former and the idealism of the latter, while the final chapter considers objections a Marxist might raise against Wittgensteinian social philosophy. The book concludes with a summary of the common approach to philosophical and methodological problems shared by Marx and Wittgenstein. The discovery of connections between humanist Marxism and Wittgenstein serves to clarify the philosophical basis of humanist Marxism while demonstrating a more radical stream of thought than is normally associated with Wittgenstein. Our aim will be to reconcile the two approaches, to establish the case for a 'Wittgensteinian Marx' and a 'progressive Wittgenstein'.

Notes

[1] Marx's unpopularity among Anglo-Saxon philosophers could be attributed to the dominance of empiricism in Anglo-Saxon thought. See C. Taylor, 'Marxism and empiricism', *British Analytical Philosophy*, edited by B. Williams and A. Montefiore (London: Routledge and Kegan Paul, 1966) pp. 227–46.

[2] A. Janik and S. Toulmin, *Wittgenstein's Vienna* (London: Weidenfeld and Nicolson, 1973) p. 19. They emphasise that despite this Anglicisation Wittgenstein's work was embedded in a strictly Germanic tradition. To some extent the same fate befell Hegel, as Gellner has observed: 'in Cambridge, Michael Oakeshott developed a water-colour variant of Hegelianism designed mainly for the preservation of the amenities and privileges of rural England'. E. Gellner, 'Hegel's last secrets', *Encounter* (April 1976), p. 34.

[3] A. Janik and S. Toulmin, *op. cit.*, p. 19.

[4] L. Wittgenstein, *Culture and Value* (Oxford: Basil Blackwell, 1980), p. 18e.

[5] See W. W. Bartley III, *Wittgenstein* (London: Quartet Books, 1974), p. 9.

[6] L. Wittgenstein, *Tractatus Logico-Philosophicus* (London: Routledge and Kegan Paul, 1961).

[7] L. Wittgenstein, *Philosophical Investigations* (Oxford: Basil Blackwell, 1968); P. Sraffa, *Production of Commodities by Means of Commodities* (Cambridge: University Press, 1960); Janik and Toulmin, *op. cit.*, compare Wittgenstein's shift in direction with Loos' architectural advances and Hoffmanstahl's rejection of lyric poetry in favour of morality plays.

[8] K. Marx, 'Economic and philosophical manuscripts', *Collected Works* III (London: Lawrence and Wishart, 1975), p. 302.

[9] K. Marx, 'On Hegel', *Collected Works* I, p. 577.

[10] G. Lukács, *History and Class Consciousness* (London: Merlin Press, 1971); L. Goldmann, *The Human Sciences and Philosophy* (London: Jonathan Cape, 1969), *Power and Humanism* (Nottingham: Spokesman Books, 1974), *Lukács and Heidegger* (London: Routledge and Kegan Paul, 1977).

[11] See, for example, L. Althusser, *For Marx* (London: Penguin, 1969); J. Hoffman, *Marxism and the Theory of Praxis* (London: Lawrence and Wishart, 1975).

I

The Marxist versus the empiricist theory of knowledge

During the twentieth century Marxism has been dominant in Europe whilst a particular form of empiricism has dominated Anglo-Saxon philosophy.[1] However, in recent years criticism of the fundamental assumptions of empiricism has emerged from *within* the Anglo-Saxon tradition as a result of the work of Wittgenstein, Austin, Ryle and Geach in philosophy and Winch in the social sciences.[2] The work of the latter has opened up the possibility of a convergence between Wittgensteinian philosophy and interpretive sociology. This has been considered, for example, by Habermas and Apel.[3] Recent work has, as we shall see, also pointed to similarities between the Wittgensteinian and Marxist approaches to the understanding of social life.[4] Although a bridge between Anglo-Saxon and European philosophy now seems possible, it is none the less true that the two approaches are, on the whole, seen as poles apart. In this chapter the relationship between the empiricist theory of knowledge and its Marxist counterpart will be explored. As we shall see, Marxism differs from both classical empiricism and classical idealism by stressing the collective and practical rather than the individualistic and contemplative aspects of knowledge.

For Marx both knowledge and ideology are social products and therefore limited by the social milieu, whereas for the empiricist the scope of knowledge is limited only by the individual's cognitive faculties. A further difference is that for the empiricists, from Locke onwards, our complex systems of knowledge are held to be ultimately derived from or analysable in terms of the contents of sense-experience.[5] Subsequent work within the empiricist tradition – while expressing wide variation – has remained true to its sensory-based model of cognition. Modern variants have conceded the possibility of the contribution of the mind but only in the form of 'innate dispositions' or 'propensities for inference'.[6] Ultimately, however, any claim to possess knowledge is referred to the allegedly infallible tribunal of personal sense-experience.

For the empiricist, cognition is essentially passive, while for the Marxist it is creative: our knowledge of the world is bound up with the activities we engage in when changing the world, the subject and object of knowledge are merely different aspects of human activity. Marx's critique of passive theories of knowledge is stated clearly in his 'Theses on Feuerbach' and in his critique of the methodological assumptions underpinning political and economic liberalism, which have their epistemological counterpart in atomistic theories which break knowledge down into its constituent elements of sense data.[7] Against the individualistic or atomistic concern with sense-experience which drives a wedge between the mind and its object, Marxism offers an historical and sociological account of the growth of knowledge, alien to empiricism.

Marx's overcoming of the subject–object distinction expressed in passive theories of knowledge has its origins in Hegelian idealism. The central role of the knowing subject in Kant's account of human knowledge bequeathed problems concerning the existence of a realm of objectivity which Hegel sought to overcome without reverting to naïve realism or Berkeleyan phenomenalism. In Hegel's work the realm of objectivity is culturally mediated by the historical milieu.[8] Subsequently, this identification of objectivity and praxis has been developed by humanist Marxists into the notion of a world-view or world-vision, a notion which has been seen as idealist in so far as it presupposes a human contribution to the determination of knowledge and sees objectivity as based on shared practices and acquired skills. In Wittgenstein's words, it 'is manifested in human action'.[9] This does not mean that the objective world is somehow unreal, for standards of objectivity, objective facts such as the movement of the planets, exist independently but our knowledge of them is only acquired as we learn to participate with others in the world. For, whilst the movement of the planets may be explained in terms of objective laws, we can only talk of it if people show in their activities and way of life that it is a meaningful utterance. The objects of knowledge may exist independently of men, but our knowledge of them is a social product. This socio-historic transcendence of the gulf between subject and object finds expression in Hegel's remark that 'Objectivity is thus, as it were, only the husk under which the concept lies concealed', a remark which suggests a notion intelligible to both Marxists and Wittgensteinians, namely, that objectivity is grounded in particular historical circumstances.[10]

The extent of Marx's debt to Hegel is, of course, a matter of intense controversy within Marxism and has divided Marx's followers. Whilst Hegel's influence is manifest throughout most of his work, the question is whether the Hegelianism of his later work represents a 'deviation' from the concerns of the mature Marx, or whether it constitutes a clearly defined commitment to Hegelianism. These problems are reflected in Marx's account of ideology for it has been suggested that a number of divergent models may be found in his writings indicating a change of direction at a certain stage of his work.

The concept of ideology in the early and later Marx

A number of models of ideology, including the conspiracy and *camera obscura* models, have been associated with Marx's earlier works.[11] The former refers to the view that ideologies are transmitted by the agencies of the dominant class into the otherwise blank minds of the working class and could be traced to Marx's comment in 'The German ideology' that:

> The ideas of the ruling class are in every epoch the ruling ideas: i.e., the class which is the ruling *material* force of society is at the same time its ruling *intellectual* force. The class which has the means of material production at its disposal, consequently also controls the means of mental production, so that the ideas of those who lack the means of mental production are on the whole subject to it. The ruling ideas are nothing more than the ideal expression of the dominant material relations, the dominant material relations grasped as ideas; hence of the relations which make the one class the ruling one, therefore, the ideas of its dominance.[12]

If Marx means here simply that ideas are pumped into the minds of the subordinate class through outside agencies, then it would seem that he is offering a conspiracy theory based on an empiricist *tabula rasa* model, in which the mind is seen as a passive receiver of information. This model is open to criticism as a very crude formulation of 'how ideology works'.[13] But it is doubtful here whether Marx is referring just to control over the means of dissemination: his point seems to be that bourgeois ideas are more effective in the sense that the dominant class reproduce their ideas by acting as if they were true. In other words, they shape reality to conform to their ideas and in that sense their ideas become the ruling ones. Rather than explicitly attributing the dominance of a particular ideology to control over the means of dissemination, Marx is merely drawing attention to the relationship between the power of the ruling class and the effectiveness of its ideas in making the world intelligible. It is possible to talk of the dominance of particular ideas without necessarily invoking deception, but instead examining the structure of capitalist society and the nature of class relationships. Where deception does enter into ideology, it may be more fruitful to talk of self-deception rather than the deliberate deception of one class by another, a point Marx stresses in the *Eighteenth Brumaire*

> But unheroic as bourgeois society is, it nevertheless took heroism, sacrifice, terror, civil war and battles of peoples to bring it into being. And in the classically austere traditions of the Roman republic its gladiators found the ideals and the art forms, the self-deceptions that they needed in order to conceal from themselves the bourgeois limitations of the content of their struggles and to keep their enthusiasm on the high plane of the great historical tragedy.[14]

The second model of ideology associated with Marx's early work is the *camera obscura* model, according to which our ideas give us an inverted picture of reality. It is formulated as follows:

> Men are the producers of their conceptions, ideas, etc., that is, real, active men, as they are conditioned by a definite development of their productive forces and of the intercourse corresponding to these, up to its furthest forms. Consciousness (*das Bewusstsein*) can never be anything else than conscious being (*das bewusste Sein*), and the being of men is their actual life-process. If in all ideology men and their relations appear upside down as in a *camera obscura*, this phenomenon arises just as much from their historical life-process as the inversion of objects on the retina does from their physical life-process.[15]

This metaphor has, however, been criticised by Mepham who objects to what he sees as the implicit assumption that each idea is the distorted representation of something to which it corresponds in an isomorphic manner:

> The view that ideology is made up of *ideas* is itself misleading to the extent that this has been taken in philosophy to suggest that the units of which ideology is composed, or out of which it is constructed, are independent of one another, and that they can be traced back to atomistic ideas which are derived from reality 'one at a time', or on a one-to-one basis ... we cannot understand ideological concepts or ideological propositions as standing in some one-to-one relation with non-ideological, non-distorted, factual or scientific concepts, propositions or facts. The translation of ideology (or manifest text) into the true underlying (latent) text cannot be performed on a word to word or proposition to proposition basis.[16]

Marx's view of an inverted reality, he argues, suggests that men's representations are mere illusions, epiphenomena or phantoms and that, therefore, ideas lack any practical effectiveness. In the light of Marx's earlier dictum that religion 'is the opium of the people', this might indicate that ideology functions as a drug which, acting on a person's cognitive and perceptual apparatus, prevents him from seeing what there is to be seen and this, in effect, reduces ideas to an uncontrollable reflex of the economic substructure. This conception of ideas as phantoms, it is argued, prevents Marx from offering a thorough analysis of the relationship between ideas and reality as provided in *Capital*.

But there are difficulties with this interpretation of the *camera obscura* and opiate metaphors. In setting out the *camera obscura* metaphor, Marx is not saying that every idea is inverted, for then we would have to question the validity of language and discourse itself as a vehicle for communication. Rather, he is grounding ideology in the form of social life in which it emerges: the way we both see and mis-see the world is rooted in our way of life. Even when comparing religion to a drug, Marx acknowledges its importance as an avenue of dissatisfaction with existing social conditions. Far from reducing ideas to mere illusions, he emphasises, like Wittgenstein (see Chapter VI), their *significance* to those who hold them, for '*Religious* distress is at the same time the expression of real distress and also the against real distress. Religion is the sigh of the oppressed creature, the heart of a heartless world, just as it is the spirit of spiritless conditions'.[17] When Marx suggests that our ideas are inverted representations of reality, he is not saying that *everything* appears upside down, but only the relationship between men and their circumstances. Ideological thought represents social life as the embodiment of certain ideas rather than seeing these ideas as arising from social life. An example here would be the idea that the principle of loyalty dominated the social life of feudalism, whilst the principle of freedom dominates the social institutions of modern capitalism and provides their *raison d'être*. What is mistaken is the assumption that social institutions are the embodiment of these principles, when, in fact, the particular modes of production give rise to specific ideas and principles. Marx's search for the source of values, ideas and beliefs within particular social formations remained a central concern throughout his work, receiving further elaboration in the *Grundrisse* and *Capital*.[18]

Nevertheless, it has been argued that Marx advances a very different account of ideology in his later work, namely, that he suggests that ideas can only be disseminated successfully because they are in some way effective in interpreting reality, for 'the effective dissemination of ideas is only possible because, or to the extent that, the ideas thus disseminated are ideas which, for quite different reasons, do have a sufficient degree of effectiveness both in rendering social reality intelligible and in guiding practice within it for them to be apparently acceptable'.[19] According to Mepham, this view prevails in *Capital* where Marx shows that the relationship between ideas and reality provides the key to the ruling ideology, that the basis of ideology lies in its apparent justification by the perceived form of social reality. To discover the underlying truth we therefore need to find out what is concealed by the apparent 'facts'. Instead of postulating a causal relationship between social and economic circumstances and ideology, Marx is saying that the social situation might be such as to 'provide a person with reasons for thinking in terms of categories which necessarily generate falsehood and illusion'.[20] Of course lies and deceptions exist, but Marx wants to go further than this, to account for the fact that ideologies make life intelligible for people. The ruling ideas are those of the ruling class because, within limits, those ideas work in so far as they seem to account for reality, to give it meaning. Social reality thus gives rise to ideas which are more than the mere illusions or phantoms which Marx described in his earlier work. On this revised theory of knowledge, the origins of ideology lie in the social reality itself, in phenomenal forms such as the wage form. Social life is organised or structured in a way that renders it opaque to its members. This opacity may be accounted for by the fact that the forms in which reality presents itself conceal the real relations which themselves produce the appearances. This distinction between phenomenal forms and the essence of social reality is developed by Marx in the context of his critique of political economy, where he tries to show that the categories used by the political economists exclude certain features of social life from consideration. Ideology cannot therefore be reduced to a collection of separate lies and illusions. Rather, it is a body or system of thought organised within a range of interdependent categories. The reason why we are not aware of these categories is that our awareness is organised through them. It follows that ideologies can only be understood by reference to the forms of social life in which they arise: we see things in a certain way because that is how they present themselves to us.

There are, however, a number of difficulties with this interpretation. To begin with there are grounds for rejecting the assumption of a radical break between the early Marx's *camera obscura* and opiate models and the mature work. Indeed, the remarks on religion in 1833, cited above, bear a close resemblance to the view Mepham attributes to the later work, in so far as they stress that religion *does* make reality intelligible to people. Furthermore, Mepham's remark that the social situation might be such as to provide a person with reasons for thinking in terms of categories which generate falsehood is also puzzling. Do we have reasons for thinking in terms of particular categories? We may have reasons for holding certain beliefs or undertaking particular actions, but we do not usually talk of having reasons for the concepts we hold. If we think of categories as the components of a world-view, then we can see the difficulty of talking in terms of reasons, for this would presuppose the possibility of choice. We do not choose between world views although we may give reasons for holding a *particular* belief. Moreover, Mepham seeks to explain the way we talk about social life in terms of the way it presents itself to us, as if the latter were independent of the former and, in doing so, he seems to commit himself to an empirical realist position. Indeed, he defends this position against the idea of a world-view which he criticises for its idealism:

> The notion of 'world-views' tends to be explained on the model of Gestalt-switch experiences of visual perception. Marx's view clearly differs from this in at least this basic respect. The difference between the one 'language' and the other is one which can be explained in terms of appearance and reality, or in terms of the aspect of reality which is its appearance and that which is its hidden substratum. Thus the

difference is explained by reference to the properties of the object and not solely of the subject and his idiosyncrasies.[21]

But to talk of world-view does not imply a concern simply with the *subjective* views of individuals. Rather it implies a reference to a whole way of life or set of activities in which people participate. In any case one can accept the point that 'Social life is a domain of meanings with which men "spontaneously" think their relations to other men and to nature' without discarding the idea of a world-view. For world-views are concerned with the properties of groups or classes rather than the individual and focus on a 'system of thought' rather than a collection of separate illusions.[22] If we talk of the way things appear from *within* a world-view we can talk of holders of different world-views seeing different things in the world or of experiencing the world differently. The idea that different forms of social life generate different ways of seeing the world is a characteristic Hegelian-Marxist notion. It contrasts sharply with the empirical realist model which excludes the possibility of different ways of representing a series of events.

It could be argued, then, that Marx advances two very different theories of knowledge: in the early work he emphasises that we are deceived by the dominant ideology and sees ideas as inverted representations of reality, making use of the *camera obscura* metaphor. The later theory of knowledge, however, is based on an essence–appearance distinction: both capitalist and worker are equally deceived by these appearances but the appearances are not merely illusions but are built into reality itself. If there is a discrepancy between the early and later accounts of ideology, which is questionable, this could be accounted for by Marx's developing interest in the genesis of ideology rather than by a radical shift of outlook. In the earlier work Marx is criticising a particular philosophical position, namely that of the Young Hegelians (see Chapter VII), whereas in *Capital* he was dissecting the structure of capitalist society. His initial interest lay in particular philosophical views and religious beliefs rather than the economic theories discussed in *Capital*. This difference in aim and subject matter may account for any divergences between the two periods, but it is certainly exaggerating these discrepancies to say that 'Marx has not, in such early works on which discussions of ideology are usually based, achieved a clear theoretical position on the origin of ideology, and that the metaphors in terms of which he discusses the problem have to be drastically modified in the light of what he says in his later works'.[23] Indeed, it could be argued that in the later work Marx develops certain aspects of the *camera obscura* metaphor by examining more thoroughly what is involved in the historical life-process. Furthermore, the reference in *Capital* to the mystification of all classes by the 'phenomenal forms' is anticipated by the 'Economic and philosophical manuscripts' where he shows how both the property owners and the propertyless are subject to the alienating and reifying effects of capitalist social relations.

Instead of fragmenting Marx's work, we need to examine his theory of knowledge as a whole. This is not to deny that there are many conflicts in his work, for example, between his emphasis on class struggle and reification, between his attempt to formulate universal laws governing the succession of social formations and his argument that each age gives rise to its own laws, as well as ambiguities in his account of the relationship between facts and values, and the role of human needs in his account of alienation. But while conflicts and contradictions do exist, we cannot employ them to postulate an absolute temporal distinction between the different periods of Marx's work, for these conflicts seem to persist throughout his work. His later writings should be seen as an extension and development of his earlier ideas, carrying with them the tensions and contradictions of the formative period. Notwithstanding these problems, humanist Marxists have sought to develop Marx's approach to epistemological questions by making use of the Hegelian notions of mediacy and immediacy.

Humanist Marxism: mediacy and immediacy

These notions are employed by, for example, Lukács, who argues that all thought is mediated in the sense that it exists within a particular cultural and historical context which colours our view of the world.[24] The use of the notion of mediacy in this way entails an acceptance of a plurality of perceptions of the world corresponding to different historical and social circumstances. One reason why Marxism is alien to empirical realism is precisely that it sees the dominant and subordinate classes as experiencing the world in different ways, and in that sense, living in different worlds. As Lukács says, society may appear to be immediately the same for both classes, in so far as they both experience the reifying effects of capitalism,

> But this does not prevent the *specific categories of mediation* by means of which both classes raise this immediacy to the level of consciousness, by means of which the merely immediate reality becomes for both the authentically objective reality, from being fundamentally different, thanks to the different position occupied by the two classes within the 'same' economic process.[25]

What is experienced for Lukács and other Hegelian Marxists, such as Sartre and Merleau-Ponty, is mediated by concepts derived from a class standpoint rather than the faculties of the individual knowing subject.[26]

The distinction between mediacy and immediacy plays such an important central role in the theories of knowledge of Hegelian Marxism that it merits further elaboration. These terms are not strictly exclusive and there are many examples where one's way of thinking may be both mediate *and* immediate. For example, in watching a sporting event on television, I may see the events more directly and immediately than the spectator who is actually present at the event even though the camera mediates between the subject and object of knowledge. So whether one can be said to perceive something mediately or immediately depends on the context in which the perception takes place. A more interesting example is of the biologist who examines a piece of tissue through a microscope and grasps immediately the process at work. His thought is also mediated in so far as to arrive at this level of 'immediate perception' he requires a knowledge of the basic ideas of the life sciences. That he can perceive immediately is made possible only through the mediation of his prior training. An example drawn from community studies may help to illustrate this point, namely, the notion of 'of course' statements employed by the Lynds in their second study of Middletown.[27] By 'of course' statements the Lynds were referring to assumptions that were accepted without question at the time: 'Is America democratic?', 'Does God exist?', 'Is monogamy the best form of marriage?'. These are the kinds of statements to which middle-class Americans at the time of the study would have answered 'Yes' without reflection. What we are dealing with here are what might be called 'natural attitudes', that is, ideas such as that it is natural to eat with a knife and fork, natural to drive on the left-hand side of the road, natural to be polite to people, natural to ascribe status and prestige to certain social classes and so on. These assumptions are immediate in so far as they appear obvious to those who hold them and reveal an unreflective mode of thought, but are mediated in so far as they are cultural. While certain ways of thinking may be said to be immediate in this unreflective sense, all thought is mediated in that it is grounded in a particular way of life, particular activities. Consequently, different forms of social life open up the possibility of different modes of thought. While we may describe the commonsense assumptions referred to above as immediate, to bring out their unreflective character we must also note that they are mediated in so far as they reflect a particular culture. Hegel argues that strictly speaking, 'There is no immediate knowledge. Immediate knowledge is where we have no *consciousness* of mediation; but it is mediated for all that'.[28]

Like many of Hegel's correlative pairs that have been developed in Marxism, the terms mediacy and immediacy have a relative meaning in the sense that the same statement can be both mediate and immediate, depending on the context in which it is examined. As Hegel says:

> One thing may be observed with reference to the immediate knowledge of God, of legal and ethical principles (including under the head of immediate knowledge, what is otherwise termed Instinct, Implanted or Innate Ideas, Common Sense, Natural Reason, or whatever form, in short, we give to the original spontaneity). It is a matter of general experience that education or development is required to bring out into consciousness what is therein contained. It was so even with the Platonic remi- and the Christian rite of baptism, although a sacrament, involves the additional obligation of a Christian upbringing. In short, religion and morals, however much they may be faith or immediate knowledge, are still on every side conditioned by the mediating process which is termed development, education, training.[29]

Any object of knowledge held to be immediate can always be shown to be a product of mediations. The implication of this is that a different system of mediations will reflect a different object of knowledge which is also capable of being immediately comprehended. Human history is characterised by the constant supersession of standards and values held to be immediately determined. The radical implications of this have been taken up by Lukács who sees the awareness of mediation as an essential precondition for the transformation of society.

In his essay on reification in *History and Class Consciousness*, he explores the 'categories of mediation' of the dominant and subordinate classes, pointing to their distinctive features. The crucial feature of the working-class world-view, he argues, is that its knowledge is essentially practical and transformative. The contradictions of capitalism are capable of an objective solution in practice and it is the task of the working class to resolve these contradictions: its consciousness must become deed, by transcending the reified laws which see social relationships as natural and unchanging. These reified forms of thought, however, are not merely modes of thought but the forms in which capitalist society is objectified. Given this, their abolition cannot be the result of thought alone, but must also entail the practical abolition of this form of social life. Only when the working class becomes aware of the possibilities for change inherent in the existing social order, can it become the subject–object whose praxis will change that society. While the immediate nature of the thought of the dominant class constitutes a limit to its understanding, the working class is forced to break through these limits and, in so far as it transcends immediacy, its thought is more scientific than the dominant class, but still mediated by its own distinctive historical standpoint.

The working class is able to arrive at this practical consciousness argues Lukács, following Marx, because it experiences the most extreme dehumanisation. As capitalism is dominated by the commodity form, the worker can only become class-conscious when he becomes aware of himself as a commodity, for in the commodity he recognises himself and his own relations with capital. The most effective weapon in his struggle against this dehumanisation is the ability to see the social totality as an historical totality, to see this dehumanisation as part of a wider social and historical process.[30] Lukács therefore sees the working class as both a commodity and a redeemer, whose destiny is to recover for man his species-being. This role is built into capitalism in the sense that the bourgeoisie has, as Marx has observed, 'forged the weapons that bring death to itself; it has also called into existence the men who are to wield those weapons – the modern working class'.[31] Capitalism, which turns man into a commodity, thereby digs its own grave. The working class is able to perform this redemptive role by becoming self-conscious, for its understanding of the reified epistemological split between subject and object of knowledge, its realisation that the object may be changed alters the relationship between the subject and object. This recognition that men make history paves the way for the possibility of social change as thought becomes practical rather than contemplative. In advancing an eschatological view of the working class, Lukács is clearly adopting an Hegelian position, seeing Hegel's absolute spirit reaching fruition in the self-consciousness of the chosen class. In this self-consciousness the schism between the subject and object of knowledge and theory and practice is overcome.

This awareness of the historical grounding of thought, so essential to Marxism, contrasts markedly with the ahistorical, atomistic and empiricist thought of the bourgeoisie.[32] While Marxism overcomes the duality of subject and object in a concrete historical situation, as men make history and are themselves the subject-matter of history, the classical economists, argues Lukács, failed to grasp the relationship between the economic and other spheres of social life as part of a totality:

> Thus bourgeois thought remains fixated on those forms which it believes to be immediate and original and from there it attempts to seek an understanding of economics, blithely unaware that the only phenomenon that has been formulated is its own inability to comprehend its own social foundations. Whereas for the proletariat the way is opened to a complete penetration of the forms of reification. It achieves this by starting with what is dialectically the clearest form (the immediate relation of capital and labour). It then relates this to those forms that are more remote from the production process and so includes and comprehends them, too, in the dialetical totality.[33]

Consequently, there is a failure to see the connection between economics and other aspects of social life such as legal, political and judicial institutions, and a tendency to accept the economic and social order as purely objective and unchanging. Reified thought is thus characterised by an inability to see events as part of a wider whole: it is unreflective, immediate and partial, abstracting phenomena from their socio-historical context, treating them in isolation as specialised units and is consequently ideological.[34] In contrast, Marxism draws attention to the effects of human action on economic laws and offers an understanding of history and society which is mediated by a grasp of the totality of social relationships from the standpoint of the class rather than the individual. The two modes of thought are thus an expression of the social and historical position of the two classes.

Lukács draws attention to the two epistemologies underpinning the world-views of the antagonistic classes. Criticising the contemplative stance of the bourgeois mind which accepts the world as given, he argues that as the bourgeois 'wishes only to know the world and not to change it he is forced to accept both the empirical, material rigidity of existence and the logical rigidity of concepts as unchangeable'.[35] During its rise to power the bourgeoisie had developed a total critique of social life, but once it achieved power the locus of its thought shifted from the class, facing a common enemy, to the individual capitalist competing with other members of the same class. The working class, on the other hand, is able to develop a dynamic view of society and history which takes as its starting-point the standpoint of the class. Lukács contrasts the contemplative thought of the individual with the transformative knowledge of the class:

> For when the individual confronts objective reality he is faced by a complex of ready-made and unalterable objects which allow him only the subjective responses of recognition or rejection. Only the class can relate to the whole of reality in a practical revolutionary way. (The 'species' cannot do this as it is no more than an individual that has been mythologised and stylised in a spirit of contemplation.) And the class, too, can only manage it when it can see through the reified objectivity of the given world to the process that is also its own fate.[36]

Lukács's emphasis on the mediation of ideas by one's class position is developed in the notion of a project favoured by Merleau-Ponty and Sartre.[37] This notion links knowledge and ideology to the social world and enables us to comprehend the experience of a class as a process which is constantly changing. Each class could be said to have a project or role to fulfil which mediates between it and the world, colouring its experiences. Merleau-Ponty therefore criticises what he calls 'objective thought' for looking at class-consciousness simply in terms of its objective characteristics. At the same time, he criticises classical idealism for reducing the existence of the worker to mere consciousness. Both approaches, he says, constitute a form of abstraction, which should be replaced by an examination of the actual conditions which produce class consciousness. As he observes:

> I am not conscious of being working class or middle class simply because, as a matter of fact, I sell my labour or, equally as a matter of fact, because my interests are bound up with capitalism, nor do I become one or the other on the day on which I elect to view history in the light of the class struggle: what happens is that 'I exist as working class' or 'I exist as middle class' in the first place, and it is this mode of dealing with the world and society which provides both the motives for my revolutionary or conservative projects and my explicit judgements of the type 'I am working class' or 'I am middle class', without its being possible to deduce the former from the latter, or *vice versa*. What makes me a proletarian is not the economic system or society considered as systems of impersonal forces, but these institutions as I carry them within me and experience them; nor is it an intellectual operation devoid of motive, but my way of being in the world within this institutional framework.[38]

> Thus to be a bourgeois or a worker is not only to be aware of being one or the other, it is to identify oneself as worker or bourgeois through an implicit or existential project which merges into our way of patterning the world and co-existing with other people ... I am all that I see, I am an intersubjective field, not despite my body and historical situation, but, on the contrary, by being this body and this situation, and through them all the rest.[39]

Merleau-Ponty's application of a genuine 'existential method' is similar to the approach taken by Sartre in his *Critique of Dialectical Reason*. The sharp delineation of class roles and the ways in which the history of a class mediates the experience of the individual member may be illustrated by his description of his observation from his window of two men, working in the garden and mending the road:

> But it would be a mistake to suppose that my perception reveals me to myself as a *man* confronted by two other *men*: the concept of man is an abstraction which never occurs in concrete intuition. It is in fact as a 'holiday-maker', confronting a gardener and road-mender, that I come to conceive myself; and in making myself what I am I discover them as they make themselves, that is, as their work produces them; but to the extent that I cannot see them as ants (as the aesthete does) or as robots (as the neurotic does), and to the extent that I have to project myself through them before their ends, in order to differentiate their ends from mine, I realise myself as a member of a particular society which determines everyone's opportunities and aims; and beyond their present activity, I rediscover their life itself, the relation between needs and wages, and, further still, social divisions and class struggles. In this way, the affective quality of my perception depends both on my social and political attitude and on contemporary events (strikes, threats of civil or foreign war, occupation of the country by enemy troops or a more or less illusory 'social truce').[40]

By using the idea of a project we can understood how thought becomes ideological as historical circumstance change. We might say the bourgeois project is correct at certain periods in so far as it enables the class to solve the problems posed by history. As it ascended, for example, its project was viable in the sense that its view of the world and of itself made it the dominant class. It was able to make its conceptions of reality *become* real by acting them out. But as it declined it came to rely on apologetics rather than science, a shift observed by Marx in 'The German ideology':

> The more the normal form of intercourse of society, and with it, the conditions of the ruling class, develop their contradiction to the advanced productive forces, and the greater the consequent discord within the ruling class itself as well as between it and the class ruled by it, the more fictitious, of course, becomes the consciousness which originally corresponded to this form of intercourse (i.e., it ceases to be the consciousness corresponding to this form of intercourse), and the more do the old traditional ideas of these relations of intercourse, in which actual private interests, etc., etc., are expressed as universal interests, descend to the level of mere idealising phrases, conscious illusion, deliberate hypocrisy. But the more their falsity is exposed by life, and the less meaning they have for consciousness itself, the more resolutely are they asserted, the more hypocritical, moral and holy becomes the language of this normal society.[41]

From the way in which the distinction between mediacy and immediacy has been construed here, it might seem analogous to the distinction between theory and observation which, according to Cohen, rests on a distinction between essence and appearance. He argues that 'there is a gulf between appearance and reality when and only when the explanation of a state of affairs renders unacceptable the description that it is natural to give of it if one lacks the explanation, this description being based purely on observation and committing the observer to no theoretical hypotheses'.[42] The implication is that a purely unreflective observation of social relationships may give a misleading impression of their true nature. But if one is capable of theorising, of going beyond unreflective observation, one is likely to arrive at a correct picture of reality. While on the surface there may seem little difference between the essence–appearance and mediacy–immediacy distinctions, using the latter, the truth we arrive at is seen as relative to the way in which we arrive at the truth. Of course the objective world can exist independently of us but what is dependent upon shared activity or praxis is our knowledge of the objective world, as the various cognitive interests underpinning our modes of thought will give rise to very different pictures of the world. On the essence–appearance model, however, our knowledge of the truth presupposes access to an external court of appeal, namely the fact experienced. The way in which we arrive at the truth, using this distinction, will not substantially determine the nature of the truth itself. This presupposes that there is an unchanging essence of reality which the working class or its representatives alone may uncover, whereas on the Hegelian-Marxist model, the nature of reality is affected by changes in the standpoint from which it is observed.

To say that thought is mediated thereby allows the possibility of other modes of thought embedded in different forms of life. The essence–appearance distinction is often attributed to the later work of Marx and is contrasted with his use of Hegelian categories in his earlier work. Given that attempts to dissociate Marx from his Hegelian heritage have relied so heavily on the essence–appearance distinction, we shall therefore analyse this distinction more thoroughly. Following an examination of the problems it raises, including the difficulties in determining the scientific content of Marxism, we will consider the alternative notion of a world-view, favoured by both Hegelian Marxists and Wittgenstein.

Notes

1 See, for example, C. Taylor, 'Marxism and empiricism'. When referring to empiricism in this work, we are referring to a theory of knowledge which is sensory-based, atomistic, passive and committed to a rigid fact–value distinction.

2 J. L. Austin, *Sense and Sensibilia* (Oxford: University Press, 1962); G. Ryle, *The Concept of Mind* (London: Penguin, 1966); P. Geach, *Mental Acts* (London: Routledge and Kegan Paul, 1957); P. Winch, *The Idea of a Social Science and its Relation to Philosophy* (London: Routledge and Kegan Paul, 1958).

3 J. Habermas, *Theory and Practice* (London: Heinemann, 1974); K.-O. Apel, *Analytical Philosophy of Language and the Geisteswissenschaften* (Dordrecht: Reidel Publishing Co., 1967); B. Premo, 'The early Wittgenstein and hermeneutics', *Philosophy Today* XVI, (spring 1972), pp. 43–65.

4 F. Rossi-Landi, 'Per un uso Marxiano di Wittgenstein', *Nuovi Argomenti* (Jan–March 1966), pp. 187–230; A. R. Manser, *The End of Philosophy: Marx and Wittgenstein* (Inaugural address: University of Southampton, 1973); T. Benton, 'Winch, Wittgenstein and Marxism', *Radical Philosophy*, XIII (spring 1976).

5 J. Locke, *An Essay Concerning Human Understanding* (London: Fontana, 1964).

6 See, for example, N. Chomsky, *Problems of Knowledge and Freedom* (London: Fontana, 1971), and B. Russell, *Human Knowledge, its Scope and Limits* (London: Allen and Unwin, 1948).

7 K. Marx, 'Theses on Feuerbach', *Marx and Engels Collected Works* V, (London: Lawrence and Wishart, 1975), pp. 6–8; *Grundrisse* (London: Pelican, 1973).

8 For a discussion of the relationship between mediacy and objectivity see Hegel's *Logic*, paragraphs 37–78. Here he distinguishes his theory of knowledge from the sensory empiricist theory of Berkeley and the critical philosophy of Kant. G. W. F. Hegel, *Enzyklopädie der philosophischen Wissenschaften* I, edited by E. Moldenhauer and Karl Markus Michel (Frankfurt am Main: Suhrkamp Verlag, 1970), English translation, *The Logic of Hegel*, trans. W. Wallace (Oxford: University Press, 1972).

9 L. Wittgenstein, *Philosophical Investigations* (Oxford: Basil Blackwell, 1968) II, xi, p. 225.

10 G. W. Hegel, *Enzyklopädie der philosophischen Wissenschaften*, I, paragraph 212.

[11] See S. M. Easton, 'Explaining ideology', *Sociological Analysis and Theory* (1976); J. Mepham, 'The theory of ideology in *Capital*', *Radical Philosophy* II, (summer 1972), pp. 12–19.

[12] K. Marx and F. Engels, 'The German ideology', *Collected Works* V, p. 59.

[13] See J. Mepham, *op. cit.*

[14] K. Marx, *The Eighteenth Brumaire of Louis Bonaparte* (Moscow: Progress Publishers, 1967), p. 11.

[15] K. Marx and F. Engels, 'The German ideology', p. 36.

[16] J. Mepham, *op. cit.*, p. 13.

[17] K. Marx, 'Contribution to the critique of Hegel's philosophy of law. Introduction', *Collected Works* III, pp. 175–6.

[18] Gould makes this clear in her analysis of the *Grundrisse*, see C. Gould, *Marx's Social Ontology* (Cambridge, Mass,: MIT Press, 1978).

[19] J. Mepham, *op. cit.*, p. 12.

[20] *Ibid.*, p. 19.

[21] *Ibid.*, p. 15.

[22] See Chapter IV below.

[23] *Ibid.*, p. 12.

[24] G. Lukács, 'Reification and the consciousness of the proletariat', *History and Class Consciousness* (London: Merlin Press, 1971), pp. 183–222.

[25] *Ibid.*, p. 150.

[26] M. Merleau-Ponty, *Phenomenology of Perception* trans. C. Smith, (London: Routledge and Kegan Paul, 1962); J.-P. Sartre, *Critique of Dialectical Reason* trans. A. Sheridan-Smith (London: New Left Books 1976).

[27] R. S. and H. Lynd, *Middletown in Transition* (New York: Harcourt Brace, 1937).

[28] G. W. F. Hegel, 'The philosophy of religion', cited in Lukács, *op. cit.*, p. 218.

[29] G. W. F. Hegel, *The Logic of Hegel*, trans. Wallace, paragraph 67.

[30] G. Lukács, 'The Marxism of Rosa Luxemburg', *History and Class Consciousness*, pp. 27–45.

[31] K. Marx and F. Engels, 'Manifesto of the Communist Party', *Collected Works* VI, p. 490.

[32] G. Lukács, 'Reification and the consciousness of the proletariat'.

[33] *Ibid.*, p. 185.

[34] G. Lukács, 'The Marxism of Rosa Luxemburg'.

[35] G. Lukács, 'Reification and the consciousness of the proletariat', p. 202.

[36] *Ibid.*, p. 193.

[37] M. Merleau-Ponty, *op. cit.*; J. -P. Sartre, *op. cit.* However, it should be noted that Lukács was highly critical of existentialism. He saw it as essentially irrational in so far as it treats 'Nothingness' as a timeless ontological principle instead of approaching it via the categories of fetishism and reification, which are peculiar to capitalist society: 'Here existentialism flows into the modern current of irrationalism. The phenomenological and ontological method seems it is true, to stand in bold contrast to the ordinary irrationalist tendencies. Are not the former "rigorously scientific," and was not Husserl a supporter of the most fanatical of logicians, Bolzano and Brentano? But even a superficial study of the method at once discloses its links with the masters of irrationalism, Dilthey and Bergson. And when Heidegger renewed Kierkegaard's efforts, the tie became even closer. This connection is more than an accidental convergence of two methods. The more phenomenology is transformed

into the methods of existentialism, the more the underlying irrationality of the individual and of being becomes the central object and the closer becomes its affinity to irrational currents of the time. Being is meaningless, uncaused, unnecessary.'
G. Lukács, 'Existentialism', *Marxism and Human Liberation* (New York: Delta, 1973), p. 255.

[38] M. Merleau-Ponty, *op. cit.*, p. 443.

[39] *Ibid.*, pp. 447–52.

[40] J.-P. Sartre, *op. cit.*, p. 101.

[41] K. Marx and F. Engels, 'The German ideology', p. 293.

[42] G. A. Cohen, 'Karl Marx and the withering away of social science', *Philosophy and Public Affairs*, I, 2 (winter 1972); a revised version is available in G. A. Cohen, *Karl Marx's Theory of History, A Defence* (Oxford: University Press, 1978).

II
Appearance and reality

Phenomenal forms

The essence–appearance distinction found in Marx's work has a long history in Western thought and can be traced to Parmenides. This distinction raises a number of problems, many of which have been noted by post-Wittgensteinian philosophers, which we will consider following an examination of its use within Marxism. According to those Marxists who hold a hard and fast distinction between appearance and reality, the working class is deceived by the appearance of social relations. A world of phenomenal forms which serves to conceal the real nature of social relations is invoked to explain this deception: ideology is a matter of being 'taken in' by these appearances while science, on the other hand, abolishes ideology by uncovering the true essence of social relations. Support for this view may be found in *Capital*:

> a scientific analysis of competition is not possible before we have a conception of the inner nature of capital, just as the apparent motions of the heavenly bodies are not intelligible to any but him, who is acquainted with their real motions, motions which are not directly perceptible by the senses.[1]

> That in their appearance things often represent themselves in inverted form is pretty well known in every science except Political Economy.[2]

> all science would be superfluous if the outward appearance and the essence of things directly coincided.[3]

'Phenomenal forms' refers to the wage form and the commodity form: the former serves to conceal the worker's creation of surplus value for the capitalist, whilst the latter hides the fact that relationships in capitalist society are relationships between people rather than things. Both are essential to the labour theory of value which distinguishes between necessary and surplus labour, labour necessary to produce the worker's own means of subsistence and labour undertaken beyond this.[4] It is in terms of this distinction that exploitation may be defined. The fundamental question a theory of ideology must answer is why the worker accepts the fact that he is working part of the day for nothing. This question may be answered by reference to the wage form and it is here we find the essence–appearance distinction entering Marx's work.

According to Marx, the reason why the worker accepts this state of affairs is that this aspect of the work relationship is *hidden* from him. If the worker is paid £100 per week for a forty-hour week, this might seem a fair wage. But the very form in which the worker is paid disguises the fact that he is creating surplus value for his employer. Hence for Marx there can be no such thing as a fair wage. In trying to understand the anomaly of 'a fair day's wage for a fair day's work', Marx postulates a distinction between appearance and reality which he claims the political economists cannot or will not grasp:

> ... in respect of the phenomenal form 'value and price of labour', or 'wages', as contrasted with the essential relation manifested therein, viz., the value and price of labour-power, the same difference holds that holds in respect to all phenomena and their hidden substratum. The former appear directly and spontaneously as current modes of thought; the latter must first be discovered by science. Classical Political Economy nearly touches the true relation of things, without, however, consciously formulating it. This it cannot so long as it sticks in its bourgeois skin.[5]

Because its theories are based on appearances, it is inevitably led into confusion and fails to comprehend the true nature of capitalist social relations. It shares this deception by phenomenal forms with the working class. Their bewitchment is expressed in their demands for 'fair wages' and the establishment of institutions to fight for this principle. By concealing the worker's unrequited labour, the wage form conceals the essential and unique characteristic of labour-power, namely its ability to create value, a property lacking in all other commodities. The categories of political economy, such as the wage form, thus have the effect of making men and their circumstances appear upside down, says Marx, making use of the inversion metaphor also employed in 'The German ideology' (see Chapter I).

The essence–appearance distinction can also be used to illustrate the differences between capitalist and feudal social relations. If we take two variables, the extraction of surplus value and the utilitarian character of human relationships, we could argue that both prevail in capitalism and feudalism.[6] But whereas the extraction of surplus value is obvious in feudal society, in capitalism it is concealed. One of the central features of feudal life was the fact that the serfs were obliged to spend a certain amount of time working for the benefit of the lord. This was apparent to all concerned, while in capitalist society the manner in which a portion of the product of the worker's labour is retained by the capitalist obscures the very fact that it *is* retained. Unlike feudal times, the working day is not divided into stretches of time for which the worker is rewarded and stretches for which he is not.[7] On the other hand, the fact that human relationships are basically utilitarian in nature was concealed in feudal society but is overt in capitalism. There are no feigned non-utilitarian ties between capitalist and worker: production relations are clearly dominated by the cash nexus. But while feudal relations may appear *prima facie* to be marked by non-economic ties of tradition and loyalty, it is actually economic necessity that holds them together. In order for feudalism to survive, one might argue, it was necessary that the subordinate class continued to believe that their relationships were conducted on a non-utilitarian basis. Capitalism eventually superseded feudalism as the true character of this relationship revealed itself. In a sense, the essence–appearance distinction could be seen as functional for the survival of a specific economic structure.

Like the wage form, the commodity form serves to conceal the essence of social relations, preventing men from seeing that the social production process rests entirely on human relationships and not on relations between things, that is, commodities. Marx points out that a table is easily understood but:

> so soon as it steps forth as a commodity, it is changed into something transcendent. It not only stands with its feet on the ground, but in relation to all other commodities, it stands on its head and evolves out of its wooden brain grotesque ideas, far more wonderful than 'table turning' ever was.[8]

Its mystical nature arises from the very fact that it is a commodity,

> ... because in it the social character of men's labour power appears to them as an objective character stamped upon the product of that labour; because the relation of the producers to the sum total of their own labour is presented to them as a social relation, existing not between themselves, but between the products of their labour. This is the reason why the products of labour become commodities, social things whose qualities are at the same time perceptible and imperceptible by the senses.[9]

Their mystical character bears no relation to their physical properties but derives from their *form* as commodities:

> There it is a definite social relation between men, that assumes in their eyes the fantastic form of a relation between things. In order, therefore, to find an analogy, we must have recourse to the mist-enveloped regions of the religious world. In that world the productions of the human brain appear as independent beings endowed with life, and entering into relation both with one another, and with the human race. So it is in the world of commodities with the products of men's hands. This I call the Fetishism which attaches itself to the products of labour, so soon as they are produced as commodities ....[10]

Just as commodities confront the producer as an independent force in the form of capital, says Marx, so land also becomes personified in the form of the landlord and similarly 'gets on its hind legs to demand as an independent force, its share of the product created with its help'.[11] Although it is true that all societies that reach the stage of commodity production and money circulation participate in this perversion, in capitalism, according to Marx, it reaches its zenith:

> this enchanted and perverted world develops still more ... Capital thus becomes a very mystic being since all of labour's social productive forces appear to be due to capital, rather than labour as such, and seem to issue from the womb of capital itself.[12]

> The whole mystery of commodities, all the magic and necromancy that surrounds the products of labour as long as they take the form of commodities, vanishes therefore, so soon as we come to other forms of production.[13]

Reification is a predominant feature of capitalist society in particular and of all societies based on the domination of one class by another. As Marx says, we find in the 'Trinity formula' of capital, land and labour, and their corollaries, interest, ground-rent and wages, the complete reification of the capitalist mode of production:

> the conversion of social relations into things, the direct coalescence of the material production relations with their historical and social determination. It is an enchanted, perverted topsy-turvy world, in which Monsieur le Capital and Madame La Terre do their ghost-walking as social characters and at the same time directly as mere things.[14]

In the commodity form the social character of labour assumes an objective character, so that the relationship of the producers to their own labour is presented to them as a relationship between products of labour. The dominance of the commodity form in capitalism engenders qualitative social change in so far as it penetrates all aspects of society and remoulds them in its own image. But, paradoxically, while the commodity form serves to mystify social relations, it is only when it becomes the dominant category that it becomes possible to grasp the true nature of economic relationships. But such an understanding for Marx, in *Capital*, lies beyond the grasp of the political economists and the working class. Accepting reified forms as the natural form of the production relation, the political economists were unable to accurately depict social relations and thus remained the prisoners of fetishism. Instead, they proclaimed the phenomenal forms as the real and thereby concealed the truth. The commodity form, peculiar to a particular historical epoch, was seen as possessing a timeless quality. To the extent that it is deceived into accepting the commodity and wage forms as natural, the working class also remains in the grip of the dominant ideology. The doctrine of commodity-fetishism thereby 'specifies those properties of Marx's object of study itself which imperiously *demand* that appearances be demolished if the reality is to be correctly grasped. It analyses the mechanisms by which capitalist society necessarily appears to its agents as something other than it really is'.[15] On these terms, the task of Marxist science is to defetishise the world of commodities, to demonstrate that what appears as an object is in reality reified human labour.

Problems arising from the essence–appearance distinction

Although one cannot deny the significance of the essence–appearance distinction within Marx's critique of capitalism, its use in his work and that of recent theorists raises a number of problems. To begin with, the essence–appearance distinction, as we noted earlier, has been construed as a distinction between theory and observation.[16] Cohen, for example, points out that 'Marx's concept of a gulf between appearance and reality depends upon an unrefined distinction between observation and theory ...'.[17] According to this view a superficial observation of social relations may give the impression that the worker receives a fair wage for his labour, but with the aid of Marxist theory one can see through the phenomenal wage form and grasp the essence of capitalist society.

The distinction between theory and observation on which this interpretation rests has been widely criticised by philosophers of science, including Kuhn, Hanson and Popper, who have all drawn attention to the fact that observations are theory-impregnated.[18] One might, however, argue that the claim that observation is theory-laden is circular, robbing a hypothesis of the possibility of testability and rigour, but this lacks plausibility. In any experiment one selects observations relative to the theory being tested, but this may. increase the rigour of the test. The choice of Luton, for example, by the authors of the *Affluent Worker* studies, was of crucial importance in testing the embourgeoisement thesis.[19] The town was chosen precisely because it was seen as the setting most favourable to the kinds of changes predicted by proponents of the thesis. If the changes could not be found in such ideal conditions, they were unlikely to be found elsewhere. So to say that an observation is theory-laden does not necessarily imply that a rigorous test is impossible.

Secondly, it is arguable that the essence–appearance account of ideology presupposes a passive and contemplative theory of knowledge as may be illustrated by Cohen's use of the 'mirage' metaphor. He points out that a knowledge of Marxist theory does not prevent one from seeing the world in terms of its appearances any more than a traveller will stop seeing mirages when he knows what they are and can explain how they arise:

> Hence the discovery of the labour theory of value does not 'dissipate the mist' through which commodity relations are observed. Those who know the theory continue to 'move about in forms of illusion' (*Gestaltungen des Scheins*). Things do not seem different to a worker who knows Marxism. He knows that they *are* different from what they continue to seem to be. A man who can explain mirages does not thereby cease to see them.[20]

The mirage metaphor is misleading, however, in so far as we have agreed criteria for testing mirages but no consensus on criteria for testing ideological thought. But even if we accept the metaphor, we effectively render Marxism redundant, for it suggests that a worker familiar with Marxist theory can still be deceived by the phenomenal forms and remain uncommitted to any action to transform the social conditions in which these ideological forms thrive. What Cohen seems to be implying is that a person can be both aware of his exploitation – as construed by the labour theory of value – and yet unaware at the same time. But to realise one's exploitation is surely to seek to become free of the stranglehold of ideology, for if ideas are to have any practical application, such knowledge must be linked to practical efforts to change social reality. This may be illustrated by reference to ordinary linguistic practice: one can refer to one's submission to ideological thought only in the past tense. While I can describe the ways in which ideological thought has dominated my thinking in the past, it is nonsensical to talk of this happening in the present without a dubious theory of false consciousness. One says 'I was a victim of ideology' but never 'I *am* a victim of ideology' since being in this state depends on one's lack of awareness. Conversely, an awareness of exploitation would release me from the grip of ideology. Thus in critically examining his own experiences, the worker may become class conscious and enter into new relationships with the members of his class. Since this gives him a different view of the world and world-views are grounded in forms of life, in acquiring class-consciousness he is relinquishing a particular form of life. His emancipation, through self-reflection, is inseparable from his estrangement, a point noted by Apel, who refers to the '*dialectical mediation* of understanding of human self-estrangement and liberation'.[21]

However, this understanding does not result in prescriptions, strategies or guidelines for future action which demonstrate the most effective way to achieve our goals, although the spurious doctrine that the 'end justifies the means' has often been falsely attributed to Marx. While critical theory serves to create a consciousness that dissolves distortion, it is retrospective in the sense that it is developed through an understanding of the past, of the relationships of domination and subordination:

> The practical consequences of self-reflection are changes in attitude which result from insight into the causalities *in the past*, and indeed result of themselves. In contrast strategic action oriented towards the future, which is prepared for in the internal discussions of groups who (as the *avant-garde*) presuppose for themselves already successfully completed processes of enlightenment, cannot be justified in the same manner by reflective knowledge.[22]

A theory which can stimulate an emancipatory consciousness can create the conditions under which systematic distortions of communication are dissolved and thereby pave the way for a genuinely *practical* discourse. Here we can note a basic similarity between humanist Marxism and Wittgensteinian social philosophy: both are interested in systematically distorted communication and both see philosophy *qua* self-reflection as a means of freeing us from the 'bewitchment of our intelligence' by language.

Because of its essentially reflexive nature, Marxism can see itself as the outcome of certain historical developments and discover the crucial role it must perform as the principal weapon of the subordinate class in its struggle against domination. But the reflexivity of Marxist thought does not mean that it is merely contemplative; on the contrary, Marx ties philosophy closely to the revolutionary practice of the working class, seeing it as its major 'spiritual weapon'. We can therefore distinguish between the contemplative theory of knowledge, implicit in the essence–appearance account, which sees members of the subordinate class as gripped by illusions even when endowed with a knowledge of Marxism, and the practical epistemology of humanist Marxism. The separation of theories of knowledge from practice was heavily criticised by Bukharin in his paper 'Theory and practice from the standpoint of dialectical materialism',[23] where he argued that such a separation leads to a somnambulistic ideology of the kind expressed in the following lines by Calderon:

> What is life? A flurry.
> What is life? An illusion.
> A shadow, a fiction,
> And the greatest good is small
> That the whole of life is a dream
> And the dreams are dreams.[24]

In his paper, given to a conference of Soviet scientists in London in the 1930s, Bukharin pointed out that:

> Both theory and practice are *steps* in the joint process of *'the reproduction of social life'*. It is extremely characteristic that from of old the question has been asked: 'How is *cognition* possible?' But the question is not asked: 'How is *action* possible?' There is 'epistemology'. But no learned men have yet thought of inventing some special 'praxeology'.[25]

> We see, consequently, that modern capitalist theories of cognition either do not deal with the question of practice altogether ... or treat of practice in the Pickwickian sense, tearing it away from the material world or from 'the highest' forms of cognition (pragmatism, conventionalism, fictionalism, etc). The only true position is held by dialectical materialism, which rejects all species of idealism and agnosticism, and overcomes the narrowness of mechanical materialism (its ahistorism, its anti-dialectical character, its failure to understand problems of quality, its contemplative 'objectivism', etc.[26]

The essence–appearance account also shares with classical empiricism the view that ideas are imposed on to the otherwise blank minds of the observer from outside, a view Popper has described as the 'bucket theory of mind', and which is also known as the *tabula rasa* model.[27] The 'bucket' in this case is ascribed to the working class who are 'taken in' by the appearances or phenomenal forms of capitalism. Such a 'phenomenalistic' account has been widely criticised in recent years for ignoring the contribution of the active mind and particularly the importance of shared linguistic rules in the acquisition of knowledge. Both Hegelian-Marxist and post-Wittgensteinian social philosophers have stressed the way in which the world is created and shaped as we come to know it. Moreover, in seeing ideas as a reflection of phenomenal forms, the essence–appearance distinction implies that ideas are an inadequate and unreliable guide to social reality. This seems to suggest a divorce between perceptions and reality and the postulation of an external or contingent relationship between ideas and social life which is alien to Marx's argument in the *Grundrisse*, where he describes 'the development of language without individuals living *together* and talking to each other' as an absurdity.[28] Language, as an expression of ideas, cannot be separated from activity for Marx, who here seems to be anticipating the Wittgensteinian argument for an internal or necessary relationship between ideas and activity, the implications of which will be considered more fully later (see Chapter VIII).[29]

A further consequence of the essence–appearance account of ideology is its emphasis on the individual's perception of phenomenal forms. Using metaphors of the individual's sensory illusion, a theory of ideology based on the essence–appearance distinction moves closer to the empiricism of Berkeley and Russell whose epistemologies were founded upon subjective sensory experience. Russell, for example, claimed that the most complex systems of knowledge or language could be reduced to individual sense-experience and stressed the importance of psychological factors in acquiring knowledge:

> Although we are doubting the physical existence of the table, we are not doubting the experience of the sense-data which made us think there was a table; we are not doubting that, while we look, a certain colour and shape appear to us, and while we

> press, a certain sensation of hardness is experienced by us. All this, which is psychological, we are not calling into question. In fact, whatever else may be doubtful, some at least of our immediate experiences seem absolutely certain.[30]

But Russell was by no means alone in grounding epistemology in subjective sense-experience. Lenin also advanced this view in 'Materialism and empiriocriticism', where he defines matter as 'A philosophical category denoting the objective reality which is given to man by his sensations and which is copied, photographed and reflected by our sensations, while existing independently of them'.[31] This theory of knowledge has been criticised from within humanist Marxism by Merleau-Ponty who comments as follows:

> In saying again that thought is a product of the brain and, through the brain, of the external reality, in taking up again the old allegory of ideas-images, Lenin thought he was going to establish the dialectic solidly in things. He forgot that an effect does not resemble its cause and that knowledge, being an effect of things, is located in principle outside its object and attains only its internal counterpart. This was to annul all that has been said about knowledge since Epicurus, and Lenin's very problem – what he called the 'gnostilogical question' of the relationship between being and thought – re-established the pre-Hegelian theory of knowledge .... This new dogmatism, which puts the knowing subject outside the fabric of history and gives it access to absolute being, releases it from the duty of self-criticism, exempts Marxism from applying its own principles to itself, and settles dialectical thought, which by its own movement rejected it, in a massive positivity.[32]

In contrast, Merleau-Ponty, as we saw earlier, would focus on the class rather than the individual in giving an account of ideology. But while Lenin was later to reject this atomistic theory, it nevertheless survives in the resurrection of the essence–appearance, theory–observation distinction advanced by Cohen and others.

Merleau-Ponty's critique of Lenin's flirtation with empiricism bears a resemblance to Wittgenstein's critique of Russell, for Wittgenstein's attack on the private language argument and the ostensive learning model undermines the foundations of the sense-data model, namely the use of the individual as the crucial factor in cognition.[33] Rejecting the idea of a private naming of sensations or private language, he instead argues that language is derived from public rules rather than private sensations and these rules depend on the possibility of being checked by others:

> Let us imagine the following case. I want to keep a diary about the recurrence of a certain sensation. To this end I associate it with the sign 'S' and write the sign in a calendar for every day on which I have the sensation. – I will remark first of all that a definition of the sign cannot be formulated. – But still I can give myself a kind of ostensive definition. – How? Can I point to the sensation? Not in the ordinary sense. But I speak, or write the sign down, and at the same time I concentrate my attention on the sensation – and so, as it were, point to it inwardly. – But what is this

> ceremony for? for that is all it seems to be! A definition surely serves to establish the meaning of a sign. – Well, that is done precisely by the concentrating of my attention; for in this way I impress on myself the connection between the sign and the sensation. – But 'I impress it on myself' can only mean: this process brings it about that I remember the connection *right* in the future. But in the present case I have no criterion of correctness. One would like to say: whatever is going to seem right to me is right. And that only means that here we can't talk about 'right'.[34]

As rules are shared expressions of social existence rather the summation of private experiences, the proverbial hermit on a desert island could not create his own private language, as the empiricists would argue, since there would be no way of checking whether or not he had made a mistake.

In treating language and knowledge as the sum of the names individuals ascribe to sensations, the Lenin of 'Empirio-criticism' and Russell represent what might be called 'epistemological private enterprise'; a position also implicit in the views of the *Robinsonaden* criticised so vehemently by Marx in the *Grundrisse*:

> The individual and isolated hunter and fisherman, with whom Smith and Ricardo begin, belongs among the unimaginative conceits of the eighteenth-century Robinsonades, which in no way express merely a reaction against over-sophistication and a return to a misunderstood natural life, as cultural historians imagine. As little as Rousseau's *contrat social*, which brings naturally independent, autonomous subjects into relation and connection, by contract, rests on such naturalism. This is the semblance, the merely aesthetic semblance, of the Robinsonades, great and small.[35]

Marx rejects the idea that the isolated individual could create his own language:

> As regards the individual, it is clear e.g. that he relates even to language itself *as his own* only as the natural member of a human community. Language as the product of an individual is an impossibility. But the same holds for property.
>
> Language itself is the product of a community, just as it is in another respect itself the presence (*Dasein*) of the community, a presence which goes without saying.[36]

Given that Marx, like Wittgenstein, rejects the empiricist assumptions of a private language, insisting on the social foundations of knowledge, it is difficult to ground his theory of knowledge in an essence–appearance distinction.

A final problem with the essence–appearance distinction is the assumption that there can be one correct way of representing the world. Marx's theory, on this model, enables us to discover *the* single reality underlying the appearances which can produce only ideologies. Fortified with Marxist theory, the working class is in a better position to arrive at the truth regarding the nature of capitalist society. Again this bears a resemblance to empiricist methodology, where scepticism regarding the essential nature of objects is generated out of conflicting sensory perceptions of the object in question. Hence Russell's table presents him with problems because he cannot decide, without favouritism, if either the physicist's or the layman's perception of the object is veridical.[37] For Wittgenstein, this was a pseudo-problem arising from the conflation of the precise observations of science and the general observations of everyday life. But once their respective 'grammars' have been elucidated the problem of an underlying reality dissolves. Similarly in social life there are a number of different ways of representing the social world depending on the standpoint of the group or class making the judgement. As Lukács says:

> it is clear that from the standpoint of the proletariat the empirically given reality of the objects does dissolve into processes and tendencies; this process is no single unrepeatable tearing of the veil that masks the process but the unbroken alternation of ossification, contradiction and movement; and thus the proletariat represents the true reality, namely the tendencies of history awakening into consciousness.[38]

Underpinning the essence–appearance distinction is the assumption that there is a realm of 'real' relations in contrast to the phenomenal forms which mislead us, an assumption heavily criticised by certain linguistic philosophers, including Wittgenstein and Austin who have drawn attention to the practical usage of language in order to dispel the assumption of a fundamental ontological distinction between appearance and reality.[39] The word 'real', as Austin shows, does not have a single unspecifiable meaning. His analysis of the various uses of 'real' undermines the appearance–reality dichotomy, the corner-stone of philosophy's claim to possess superior insight into the nature of things. This dichotomy is also incompatible with Wittgenstein's point that the meaning of a word is determined by the various contexts in which it is employed. Given that the criteria for distinguishing the real from the non-real cannot be final, the assumption that there is a clear-cut real world in contrast to the phenomenal world, presupposed by the essence–appearance distinction, is consequently hard to maintain. Problems also arise from the further distinction between science and ideology following from the essence–appearance distinction. The use of theory, *qua* science, is seen as the means of acquiring a correct understanding of reality, since it strips away the outward appearances of social life and thereby grasps their essence. But such a criterion of demarcation between science and non-science is beset by the problems facing all philosophers of science who seek to formulate such a criterion.[40] But if we accept that not all disputes are resolvable by reference to a neutral/correct description, does this entail a Protagorean relativism? Clearly not, for even if there were no final court of appeal, this would not mean that all modes of cognition were equally acceptable. The choice is not between an authoritarian monism or an anarchic relativism but, as we shall see later, there are limits to relativism and conventionalism in the practice of everyday life (Chapters V and VI).

In the light of these problems, it would seem that the essence–appearance distinction *per se* is difficult to accept as the basis of the Marxist theory of knowledge. Apart from the difficulties inherent in the distinction, one can also point to certain features of Marx's work which suggest that he was highly critical of the contemplative theories of knowledge of his time, offered, for example, by the Young Hegelians. For Marx, in contrast, philosophical problems were essentially practical questions:

> The question whether objective truth can be attributed to human thinking is not a question of theory but is a practical question. Man must prove the truth, i.e., the reality and power, the this-worldliness of his thinking in practice. The dispute over the reality or non-reality of thinking which isolates itself from practice is a purely scholastic question.[41]

This essentially Hegelian approach is developed by Lukács who, in his work on reification, stresses the internal relationship between class consciousness and political action.[42] When the worker becomes aware of himself as a commodity his knowledge is practical in the sense that it changes both the subject and object of knowledge, overcoming the schism between the two. Once it is recognised that relationships between things are social relationships, it is possible to recognise the fetishistic character of every commodity and this consciousness itself is transformed into political action through praxis. Lukács is here expressing Hegel's point that alienation may be overcome through understanding the world and seeing its rational aspect. It follows from this that the distinction between theory and practice can also be transcended:

> *The chief significance of this type of knowledge is that the mere fact of knowledge produces an essential modification in the object known: thanks to the act of consciousness, of knowledge, the tendency inherent in it hitherto now becomes more assured and vigorous than it was or could have been before.* A further implication of this mode of knowledge, however, is that the distinction between subject and object disappears, and with it, therefore, *the distinction between theory and practice.* Without sacrificing any of its purity, impartiality or truth, theory becomes action, practice. To the extent to which knowledge, as the consciousness of the known object, imparts greater vigour and assurance to the natural development of that object than would have been possible without it, it has already and in the most immediate fashion involved itself in immediate practical action, in the transformation of life through action.[43]

This self-consciousness affords both the possibility of an understanding of capitalism and a transformation of capitalist society through praxis.

Nevertheless, Marx does make use of the essence–appearance distinction in the labour theory of value, thereby paving the way for a passive, mechanistic theory of the human subject which stresses exploitation rather than *resistance* to exploitation and devalues the importance of the class struggle. This theory could also be challenged on the grounds that the process of reification can never be fully realised. As Lukács has observed, 'This rationalisation of the world appears to be complete: it seems to penetrate the very depths of man's physical and psychic nature. It is limited, however, by its own formalism'.[44] An advanced industrial society requires an extraordinarily high degree of skill and self-determination in order to guarantee its own reproduction. If it relied on 'programmed robots' it would soon collapse, a point made more recently by Cardan who argues that too great an emphasis on reification overlooks the ability and determination of the working class to resist the processes of dehumanisation within capitalist society:

> Reification, although a fundamental tendency of capitalism, can never completely fulfil itself. If it were ever to do so, if capitalism were ever successful in transforming people into things driven only by economic forces, the system would collapse. And it wouldn't be 'in the long run' but instantly. The struggle of people against reification is, just as much as the tendency to reification, an essential condition for the functioning of capitalism. A factory in which the workers would really and totally be mere cogs of the machines, blindly carrying out managerial instructions, would stop in next to no time. Capitalism can only function by using the genuinely human activity of its subjects, which activity capitalism at the same time seeks constantly to limit and to dehumanize as much as possible. The system can only function if its fundamental tendency, which is indeed the tendency to reification, is *not* achieved. It can only function if its norms are constantly challenged in their application. The fundamental contradiction of capitalism lies here.[45]

Although the essence–appearance distinction plays an important role in Marxist economics, it seems to undermine Marx's essentially transformative epistemology. Nevertheless, this quasi-empiricist distinction has survived uneasily in the work of many of Marx's successors, largely because of its claim that Marxism offers a scientific account of social processes which penetrates the deceptive phenomenal forms to uncover the underlying structure of reality. As an account of ideology, it has been shown to be unsatisfactory, but if the Marxist critique of ideology does not rest on this distinction, what becomes of its claim to be scientific? In the following chapter we shall therefore consider the scientific status of Marxism, before moving on to an examination of the explanation of ideological beliefs in terms of the world-views of ascending and declining classes rather than by reference to phenomenal forms. The advantage of the notion of a world-view, as we shall see, is that it allows for an internal relationship between ideas and social life and relates the growth of knowledge directly to social change. Moreover, unlike the essence–appearance distinction, it allows for a plurality of perspectives rather than a single set of truths.

Notes to Chapter II

[1] K. Marx, *Capital* I (Moscow: Foreign Languages Publishing House, 1961), p. 316.

[2] *Ibid.*, p. 537.

[3] K. Marx, *Capital* III, p. 797.

[4] K. Marx, 'Wages, price and profit', *Marx and Engels: Selected Works* I (Moscow: Foreign Languages Publishing House, 1962), p. 420.

[5] K. Marx, *Capital* I, p. 542.

[6] See G. A. Cohen, 'Karl Marx and the withering away of social science', *Philosophy and Public Affairs* II (1972), pp. 182–203; a revised version is available in *Karl Marx's Theory of History, A Defence* (Oxford: Clarendon Press, 1978), pp. 326–44.

[7] For a discussion of changing conceptions of time in the transition to capitalism, see E. P. Thompson, 'Time, work discipline and industrial capitalism', *Past and Present* (Dec. 1967).

[8] K. Marx, *Capital* I, p. 71.

[9] *Ibid.*, p. 72.

[10] *Ibid.*, p. 72.

[11] K. Marx, *Capital* III, p. 804.

[12] *Ibid.*, p. 806.

[13] K. Marx, *Capital* I, p. 76.

[14] K. Marx, *Capital* III, p. 809.

[15] N. Geras, 'Marx and the critique of political economy', *Ideology in Social Science*, ed. R. Blackburn (London: Fontana, 1962), p. 286.

[16] G. A. Cohen, *op. cit.*

[17] *Ibid.*, p. 200.

[18] N. R. Hanson, *Patterns of Discovery* (Cambridge: University Press, 1958); T. S. Kuhn, *The Structure of Scientific Revolutions* (Chicago: University Press, 1962); K. Popper, 'Conjectures and refutations', *Conjectures and Refutations* (London: Routledge and Kegan Paul, 1963).

[19] J. H. Goldthorpe, D. Lockwood, F. Bechhofer, J. Platt, *The Affluent Worker in the Class Structure* (Cambridge: University Press, 1969).

[20] G. A. Cohen, *op. cit.*, p. 188.

[21] K. -O. Apel, 'The *A Priori* of communication', *Man and World* (1971), p. 35.

[22] J. Habermas, *Theory and Practice* (London: Heinemann, 1974), p. 39.

[23] N. I. Bukharin, 'Theory and practice from the standpoint of dialectical materialism', *Science at the Crossroads* (London: Frank Cass & Co., 1971), pp. 11–33.

[24] Que es la vida? Un frenesí:
Que es la vida? Una illusion,
Una sombra, una ficcion,
Y el mayor bein es psequeño,
Que toda la vida es sueño,
Y los sueños sueño son.

Calderon, 'La Vida es Sueño', *Las Comedies del Celebre Poeta Español, Don Pedro Calderon de la Barca* (Zuickavia: Libreria de los hermanos, Schumann, 1819), cited in Bukharin, *op. cit.*, pp. 16–17.

[25] N. L. Bukharin, *op. cit.*, p. 14.

[26] *Ibid.*, p. 15.

[27] K. Popper, 'The bucket and the searchlight: two theories of knowledge', *Objective Knowledge* (Oxford: University Press, 1972).

[28] K. Marx, *Grundrisse* (London: Penguin, 1973), p. 84.

[29] See P. Winch, *The Idea of a Social Science and its Relation to Philosophy* (London: Routledge and Kegan Paul, 1958), Chapter 5.

[30] B. Russell, *The Problems of Philosophy* (Oxford: University Press, 1967), p. 7.

[31] V. I. Lenin, 'Materialism and empirio-criticism', *Collected Works* XIV (Moscow: 1960–70), p. 130.

[32] M. Merleau-Ponty, *Adventures of the Dialectic* (London: Heinemann, 1974), p. 60.

[33] L. Wittgenstein, *Philosophical Investigations* (Oxford: Basil Blackwell, 1968).

[34] *Ibid.*, 258.

[35] K. Marx, *Grundrisse* (London: Penguin, 1973), p. 83.

[36] *Ibid.*, p. 490.

[37] Russell observes that 'When in ordinary life, we speak of *the* colour of the table, we only mean the sort of colour which it will seem to have to a normal spectator from an ordinary point of view under usual conditions of light. But the other colours which appear under other conditions have just as good a right to be considered real; and, therefore, to avoid favouritism, we are compelled to deny that, in itself, the table has any one particular colour.' B. Russell, *op. cit.*, p. 3.

[38] G. Lukács, 'Reification and the consciousness of the proletariat', *History and Class Consciousness*, p. 199.

[39] L. Wittgenstein, *op. cit.*; J. L. Austin, *Sense and Sensibilia* (Oxford: University Press, 1962).

[40] Popper, for example, favours a criterion of demarcation which focuses on the falsifiability and non-falsifiability of theories. Whilst he rejects the essence–appearance distinction as 'bordering on metaphysics', his own criterion could be seen as equally metaphysical. Feyerabend has therefore criticised attempts to construct absolute principles of demarcation, favouring instead 'epistemological anarchism'. K. Popper, *Conjectures and Refutations; The Logic of Scientific Discovery* (London: New Left Books, 1975).

[41] K. Marx, 'Second thesis on Feuerbach', *Collected Works* V, p. 6.

[42] G. Lukács, *op. cit.*

[43] G. Lukács, 'Tactics and ethics', *Political Writings 1919–1929* (London: New Left Books, 1972) p. 15.

[44] G. Lukács, 'Reification and the consciousness of the proletariat', p. 101.

[45] P. Cardan, *History and Revolution* (London: Solidarity, 1971), p. 4.

III
Facts and values

The essence–appearance account of ideology is committed to the view that Marxism is a science which grasps the real nature of social relations.[1] But if the essence–appearance account is itself open to criticism, it would seem that the view of Marxism as a science is also undermined. Yet if we deny Marxism scientific status, what status does it possess? Is Marxism an expression of values rather than a statement of facts? This question arises because Marxism is not just an account of how things are in capitalist society but it also appears to contain guidelines for the activity of the working class. Various accounts of the status of Marxism have been advanced but a question underpinning many of them is whether the facts of social life provide us with logically compelling reasons for accepting one course of action rather than another. This can only be answered by reference to the relationship between facts and values, between Marx's analysis of capitalism and his recommendations for change. Unlike the empiricists, Marx was not particularly concerned with the relationship between facts and values *per se* but his account of certain features of capitalist society does suggest a particular view of the relationship between description and prescription which fits neither the conventional scientific nor the ethical models.

The two-dimensional view

Although the fact–value distinction has a long ancestry in empiricist thought, an analysis of the relationship between description and prescription in social philosophy is normally associated with Weber, for whom values are *not* logically entailed by the facts.[2] In his dispute with other members of the *Verein für Sozialpolitik*, Weber argued that it was possible to distinguish statements of social policy from social scientific statements and present them separately in the *Verein*'s journal. Accepting that values were essentially a matter of individual choice and decision, Weber argued that it was impossible for science to establish which values we should adopt. It can only show us the best means to achieve particular values, their internal consistency and the effects of adopting them. But ultimately Weber saw the question of which values we should follow as a matter for individual conscience.[3]

The contingency of facts and values, expressed by Weber, also finds expression in various interpretations of Marxism. Accordingly it has been held that Marxism is scientific in so far as it attempts to establish causal relationships between certain aspects of capitalism and to formulate laws in an objective fashion. Values do not enter into this analysis. At the same time Marxism analyses reality from the point of view of the working class. In this sense it is a revolutionary ideology as well as a science but the relationship between the two is contingent and external rather than necessary and internal. The values characteristic of Marxism are not implicit in the Marxist analysis of capitalism and the commitment to socialism cannot be derived from an objective observation of the facts. Commitment requires a decision on the part of the individual or group. This interpretation seems to suggest that a knowledge of Marxism would not necessarily lead to a different view of the world. Even the worker using the labour theory of value, who is able to perceive the real nature of capitalism, may continue to be impressed by the phenomenal forms, just as we continue to be taken in by mirages when we understand how they work, to use Cohen's example.[4] No conclusion is logically entailed by the knowledge of the facts – the assumption is that a further step is necessary.

The one-dimensional view I: Marxism as a science

In contrast to the dualistic interpretation, the monistic approach rejects the fact–value distinction. It can, as we shall see, take various forms. One expression of this view may be found in Engels' attempt to ground all aspects of Marxism, including statements about the merits of socialism, on a scientific basis. We find this in his preface to *Socialism: Utopian and Scientific* where he compares Marx's ideas with those of the Ricardian socialists and in 'The condition of the working class in England' where his description of social life embodies Marxist values.[5] Marx's *Capital* is seen by Engels as an objective causal analysis of capitalism in which Marx seeks to establish causal connections and to formulate laws, such as the law of value, in a scientific fashion. It follows from this conception of Marxism that workers presented with the facts will realise their exploitation and revolt. As Engels says:

> The materialist conception of history starts from the proposition that the production of the means to support human life and, next to production, the exchange of things produced, is the basis of all social structure; that in every society that has appeared in history, the manner in which wealth is distributed and society divided into classes or orders is dependent upon what is produced, how it is produced, and how the

> products are exchanged. From this point of view, the final causes of all social changes and political revolutions are to be sought, not in man's brains, not in man's better insight into eternal truth and justice, but in changes in the modes of production and exchange. They are to be sought not in the *philosophy*, but in the *economics* of each particular epoch. The growing perception that existing social institutions are unreasonable and unjust, that reason has become unreason and right wrong, is only proof that in the modes of production and exchange changes have silently taken place with which the social order, adapted to earlier economic conditions, is no longer in keeping. From this it also follows that the means of getting rid of the incongruities that have been brought to light must also be present, in a more or less developed condition, within the changed modes of production themselves. These means are not to be invented by deduction from fundamental principles, but are to be discovered in the stubborn facts of the existing system of production.[6]

Engels is thus able to account for the inevitability and desirability of socialism without making any reference to the values, aims and purposes of individuals and groups. Instead he refers to the internal contradictions of capitalism such as the conflict between the forces and relations of production which inevitably weaken the society. In this sense Engels equates 'scientific Socialism' with a knowledge of the facts of capitalist development rather than a commitment to specific values such as justice and freedom. The desirability of socialism is incorporated into these facts:

> To accomplish this act of universal emancipation is the historical mission of the modern proletariat. To thoroughly comprehend the historical conditions and thus the very nature of this act, to impart to the now oppressed proletarian class a full knowledge of the conditions and of the meaning of the momentous act it is called upon to accomplish, this is the task of the theoretical expression of the proletarian movement, scientific Socialism.[7]

Engels firmly rejects an analysis of capitalism in terms of ethical problems and the possible solutions to those problems. Indeed even his notion of exploitation is used in a technical rather than ethical sense to refer to the distinction between necessary and surplus labour. However Engels' approach is problematic since it seems to rest on the assumption that there is ultimately one correct way of seeing the world, one correct set of facts which, as we shall see, is alien to Marx's work. Against Engels' account of Marxism as a system of natural descriptions having a moral content, one could argue that each class has its own account of the natural facts. Just as values are explicable only in terms of changing modes of human activity so are the facts which are inextricably linked to them. Whilst Engels is correct to conflate facts and values, he wrongly assumes that there is only one way that they can be conflated.

The one-dimensional view II: Marxism as a moral theory

The other side of the coin is a one-dimensional view which emphasises the role of prescriptions within Marxism. Debates concerning the question of whether Marx's theory is a moral theory flourished in the 1960s following the discovery of the 'Economic and philosophical manuscripts'. Critics of Stalinism within communist countries sought to identify Marxism with a moral theory. Previously it had been accepted within the communist bloc that Marxism was a science, strictly analogous to the natural sciences. Challenges to this view focused on the possible alternative of a Marxist ethics. In the context of this debate one should note that attempts have been made recently to revive a 'positivistic' conception of Marxism in the face of the development of Marxist humanism. Hoffmann, for example, reaffirms a positivistic approach when he criticises the expression of this new movement within Marxism in the spontaneous emergence of workers' councils in Hungary in 1956.[8] Arguments for a Marxist ethics range from the view that the intrusion of values into Marx's analysis, although undeniable, is unacceptable, to the idea that an ethical approach is the appropriate basis for Marx's description of capitalism.

(a) *Evaluative historicism*

Popper, for example, argues that although Marx's values do enter into his analysis of how things are in capitalist society, they should be excluded.[9] This reduction of description to prescription is illegitimate. Whilst he acknowledges a theoretical contribution to any descriptive language, he shares Weber's aversion to the inclusion of any evaluative content. Accordingly he treats Marxism as little more than propaganda designed to advance the interests of a particular class, having no scientific basis. He sees in the writings of both Marx and Hegel grand systems of metaphysical ideas that are not grounded in the realities of social life, illicitly attempting to give a total interpretation of history and society which may then be used to justify large-scale social change. It is this metaphysically-orientated intrusion of values into Marxism which Popper labels 'historicism', and on these grounds Marxism is dismissed as a pseudo-science. Although sympathetic to Marx's humanistic goals of reducing human misery and increasing human freedom, he argues that these values have no part to play in a science of society. Moreover, the effect of these values has led Marx's followers to take a highly uncritical stance when confronted with possible evidence against Marx's theory. He claims that they 're-interpreted both the theory and the evidence in order to make them agree. In this way they rescued the theory from refutation; but they did so at the price of adopting a device which made it irrefutable. They thus gave a conventionalist twist to the theory; and by this strategem they destroyed its much-advertised claim to scientific status'.[10] In effect Marx's evaluative historicism, concludes Popper, destroys the scientific claims of Marxism, thereby rendering the theory non-falsifiable.

(b) *Marxism as a morality*

A number of views have been advanced which stress the legitimacy of the evaluative content in Marx's work. Marxism is seen primarily as a utopian and idealistic theory rather than a science, representing and advancing the interests of the proletariat. It follows from this that communism is seen as morally superior to capitalism. Taylor, for example, argues that Marxism should be seen as a moral theory and distinguishes between Marxism and 'traditional British empiricism' in terms of their respective views of the fact–value distinction.[11] Marx is committed to certain ethical standards, he says, in so far as he sees communist society as constituting a better society than our own, on the grounds that it will allow for self-realisation. But this moral view is at the same time grounded in certain facts about human beings. For example, Marx's theory of human nature, as outlined in the 'Paris manuscripts' sees men as species-beings which presupposes certain assumptions regarding human needs. Marx therefore concludes that capitalist society is incapable of reconciling man to his species-being and man is alienated and dehumanised by capitalism. Communist society, by contrast, will fulfil these basic human needs. Built into Marx's account, argues Taylor, are certain undeniable moral conclusions, namely that having recognised these needs, men will attempt to realise them. It is in this sense Taylor speaks of a Marxist *morality*, by which he means a doctrine concerned with the 'fundamental human good and the way to realize it ...'.[12] A classless society is a universal good since it will allow for greater self-actualisation than in capitalism. This moral judgement is founded on a particular fact, namely what Marx sees as the human essence. Judgements concerning the way men ought to live or how societies should be organised may be justified by reference to human nature and human needs. In this way facts and values, description and prescription, are intertwined. But the relationship is internal rather than contingent.

A similar view has been advanced by Gould who sees Marx's critique of capitalism as primarily a normative one predicated on the principles of freedom and justice.[13] She argues that while the process of exchange between capitalist and worker is just in the sense that it is a free process and the agents are reciprocally related, in the production process relations are unfree, unequal and therefore unjust. Capitalism thus fails to meet its own abstract principle of justice as embodied in the exchange relation. But it is also unjust in the more general sense of depriving men of their freedom since it fails to allow for the 'mutuality of social relations' whereby men recognise the capacity of others for freedom and seek to enhance each other's freedom. Instead, within capitalism, men treat each other instrumentally, merely as a means to an end. The principle of justice demands an equal relationship allowing for the promotion of self-realisation, which is the essence of freedom. Gould therefore sees Marx as sharply distinguishing capitalism and communism on the principle of justice: the central value of communism is 'positive freedom' which ensures full mutuality. Gould sees Marx's morality as following inevitably from his ontology: the capacity for self-transformative activity is possessed by all human beings and is, therefore, universal. However, she is careful to point out that this does not entail a 'fixed nature' since men themselves freely create their natures.

In using Marx's account of human needs as a point of comparison between capitalism and communism, Taylor and Gould run into difficulties, as we shall see, in relating this 'transcendental' approach to Marx's own emphasis on the relativity of standards of justice to particular epochs. One may also note that although Taylor sees Marx's rejection of the fact–value distinction as typically Hegelian and therefore alien to Anglo-Saxon thought, this is not wholly correct since Geach, Anscombe and Foot, among other Anglo-Saxon philosophers, accept that certain facts entail certain values and that description and evaluation cannot be separated.[14]

Whilst Taylor and Gould see human needs as serving as an external criterion by means of which different societies may be judged, Allen suggests that the principle of utility provides this criterion.[15] He argues that according to Marx capitalism is unjust with the bourgeois concept of justice being inferior to that of communism. Conversely socialism is held to be just since it is founded on the principle that each gives according to his ability and receives according to his needs. Capitalist and communist modes of production may be compared in terms of the principle of utility which demands the greatest satisfaction of human needs and desires. On this principle socialist society rates better than capitalist society. In so far as the principle of utility is external to both communism and capitalism, constituting an Archimedean point against which each may be judged, it performs a similar role to Taylor's notion of trans-cultural human needs. All three therefore see Marx as arguing that communism is morally superior to capitalism.

But the textual evidence to support Allen's assignment of Marx to the utilitarian camp is far from convincing. Marx certainly had little respect for utilitarianism, as we can see from his attacks on English liberalism, particularly his acid remarks on Bentham. The following passage where he refers to the view, held by Bentham, of capital as a fixed magnitude is typical: 'But this prejudice was first established as a dogma by the arch-Philistine, Jeremy Bentham, that insipid, pedantic, leather-tongued oracle of the ordinary bourgeois intelligence of the 19th century'.[16] For Bentham's utilitarianism, as Marx was fully aware, was steeped in the values of Victorian society.

A more telling objection to Allen's view is that the principle of utility depends on the existence of certain needs that are, according to Marx, only explicable in specific forms of social life. To talk of societies being comparable in terms of the principle of utility commits one to a specification of the needs which that society meets or fails to meet. If a utilitarian principle is to provide the basis of trans-cultural criticism, it requires a transcendental theory of unchanging human needs. One can then decide how adequately this or that institution can fulfil those needs. But it is doubtful whether Marx did hold such a theory of needs since he emphasises in his attack on the 'Robinson Crusoe' model favoured by the political economists that human needs cannot be understood apart from their social context.[17]

Of the various views we have considered, the one-dimensional approach seems *prima facie* the most acceptable in so far as it accords with the Hegelian-Marxist transcendence (*Aufgehebung*) of the description–prescription dichotomy. However each of the monistic views presented here raises problems. As we have seen, Engels' account of Marxism as a science is inadequate in so far as it presupposes that there is one correct way of viewing the world. But the view of Marxism as a moral or ethical theory is also unacceptable since it is difficult to establish that Marx holds an external standard against which different modes of production can be evaluated. While defending the view that Marx legitimately combines evaluation and description in his work, one does not have to accept that this commits him to an ethical or moral theory. For instead of offering a moral standard which the ideal society must meet, Marx instead argues that each epoch has its own standards of right and justice and in this sense he offers a sociological account of morality. His approach is humanistic in so far as he focuses on human action or praxis, but he avoids the location of morality in the human essence. For Marx then, unlike Taylor and Gould, it follows that there can be no Archimedean standpoint against which different modes of production may be measured. As well as rejecting absolute moral principles, he also rejects a 'decisionist' or individualist account of morality which sees values as stemming from individual wills. Hence in setting out the rudiments of historical materialism in 'The German ideology', Marx argues:

> This conception of history thus relies on expounding the real process of production – starting from the material production of life itself – and comprehending the form of intercourse connected with and created by this mode of production, i.e., civil society in its various stages, as the basis of all history; describing it in its action as the state, and also explaining how all the different theoretical products and forms of consciousness, religion, philosophy, morality, etc., etc., arise from it, and tracing the process of their formation from that basis.[18]

At the same time Marx does offer a critique of capitalism *as a whole* but he does not undertake this from the standpoint of either absolute principles or individual conscience. Instead he arrives at his critique through a rigorous knowledge of the internal structure of capitalist society. Consequently Marx's quasi-relativist or sociological position does not lead to an acceptance of capitalist society. To see each society as containing its own legal and juridical institutions and values does not rule out criticism any more than Winch's rejection of Evans-Pritchard's account of Zande society leads him to endorse witchcraft and sorcery.[19] In both cases, as we shall see later, what is important is to be clear on what is being criticised, what kinds of criticism are relevant. Understanding a mode of production in its own right, without bringing in external principles, by understanding how different parts of the society relate to each other, is an essential precondition of developing a critique. In rejecting both extremes, Marx seems to be anticipating certain developments in Wittgensteinian philosophy which see moral judgements as intelligible only in terms of the moral practice to which the person making the judgement belongs.

Moral practices

These developments are expressed in the work of two Wittgensteinians, Phillips and Mounce, in their papers 'Does it pay to be good?' and 'On morality's having a point' which were subsequently elaborated in *Moral Practices.*[20] They point out that in certain cases it is difficult to distinguish prescriptive and descriptive elements. To call someone a liar or a thief is both to describe and condemn him. Where we wish to use these words without the evaluative element, we are obliged to qualify our use of the terms by, for example, justifying the actions of the person involved.[21] When concepts such as 'theft' and 'mendacity' are employed, they do have negative overtones but they may occasionally be used with admiration. This can be illustrated, for example, by the reverence of the press for Nixon during the Watergate affair. Although many were shocked by the revelations, others were fascinated by the web of lies spun by the President. Given the popularity of literature which glorifies *Realpolitik*, we can see that many people have more than a sneaking admiration for deceit and double- dealing in certain circumstances.

Phillips and Mounce employ Wittgenstein's technique of referring to the way in which children learn language to illustrate how values are acquired. In learning how to use terms such as 'liar', 'murderer', the child absorbs a particular evaluation of liars and murderers. A child does not first learn a set of theory-neutral facts to which values are added at a later stage of its development. Instead both facts and values are intertwined from the start. In developing this view of facts and values, Phillips and Mounce take issue with the standpoints of Hare and Foot.[22]

For Hare, morality is a matter for the individual's own conscience and cannot be entailed by the facts. In this sense he is committed to the fact–value distinction since he argues that it is possible to describe lying, for example, in a purely factual way. We could, he says, refer to lying as X-ing and attribute the additional evaluative element ourselves. Value-judgements, for Hare, arise from a general principle that the individual has ultimately decided upon himself. It follows that if one decides that in general X-ing is wrong, one can also deduce that a particular case falling under this principle is also wrong. A prescriptive conclusion is thus deduced from a prescriptive premise – one appeals from one prescriptive judgement to another and not to the facts.

For Phillips and Mounce, in contrast, moral principles do not stand in isolation from the facts but are acquired in the ability to actively participate in a shared lingustic productive community. Value judgements like lying, cheating, or 'shoddy workmanship' are not labels one attaches to a realm of facts, but are concepts acquired as we learn to participate in shared forms of life. Moral decisions are not taken with reference to universal principles which originate in subjective decisions. One does not decide that shoddy workmanship is immoral by reference to a subjective decision that has been universalised into a general rule. In so far as practical skills are acquired in a public context, the value judgements are contained within the use of those skills.

Foot, on the other hand, emphasises facts rather than decisions. Like Engels, she avoids the appeal to subjective conscience, but she also shares with Engels the view referred to earlier that a given fact necessitates the same conclusion for everyone, regardless of the moral practice to which one might belong. But Phillips and Mounce move closer to Marx in arguing that an apparently similar set of facts may entail different moral conclusions for different individuals or groups. An identical response could only be possible in a society in which there was one single moral practice. Consider, for example, the violent scenes in the black African township of Soweto in the late 1970s. A white observer might see them as a lesson to reinforce the army and police and to take further measures against the black population. A sympathiser with the townspeople may see the police action as repression to be combated before a peaceful solution is possible. In other words, the coalescence of prescription and description varies according to each moral practice: the facts inevitably incorporate certain evaluative elements derived from the moral practice to which one belongs. But to acknowledge the existence of a plurality of moral practices does not rule out the possibility of criticism. One can accept the significance of the various factual–evaluative explanations to each group while denying the competing explanations equal moral status (See Chapter VI). Apartheid, for example, is perfectly intelligible within the religious conceptions of the Dutch Reformed Church in South Africa, but in acknowledging this one is not making a commitment to that set of values. The critique of the fact–value distinction and the notion of a moral practice found in the work of Phillips and Mounce can be usefully applied to Marxism in the following two ways: firstly, we shall consider the nature and functions of terms such as 'servitude' in Marx's work and secondly we shall examine the relationship between the concept of a moral practice and Marx's idea of a mode of production.

Marxism and moral practices

(a) *'Servitude': scientific description or moral evaluation?*

Words such as 'servitude' and 'exploitation', one could argue, have a role in our language analogous to that performed by terms such as 'liar', 'thief' and 'shoddy work', in so far as each embraces both factual and evaluative elements and that these elements are internally related. One cannot accept servitude and exploitation as desirable states of affairs, without qualifying or justifying them in some way. For Engels, as we saw earlier, exploitation was a technical term used to describe the relationship between capitalist and worker. But it could also be seen as expressing certain values. To use the concept in the context of Marx's theories of surplus value is to understand what is wrong with an economic and political system. Just as one acquires the appropriate values in learning the correct use of the word 'liar', so one can grasp the nature of capitalist society as one learns the correct usage of concepts such as 'servitude', 'pauperisation', 'ruling class', 'alienation' and 'surplus value'. But although Marx uses exploitation in this technical sense it usually coincides, as Arneson has noted, with wrongful exploitation which exists firstly, when non-producers have more power than producers and is for the purpose of technical exploitation and secondly, when technical exploitation establishes an unequal distribution of economic advantages, which cannot be attributed to greater deservingness.[23] Exploitation could thus be defined as forced drudgery combined with an unequal distribution of goods, being achieved through inequalities of wealth and power.

The difference between the approaches of Wittgensteinians and Marxists here is that for the former one learns how to use terms such as 'thief', 'liar' and so on in the course of conforming to society, whilst Marx held that terms like 'servitude' are acquired in learning how to transform society. But both share the view that moral concepts are acquired in human activity, in practice, rather than in the speculations of philosophy.

Servitude and alienation are used frequently by Marx in his critique of capitalism. But the reasons for his rejection of capitalism are contained within his description of capitalist society which refers to processes of exploitation and pauperisation. Marx never felt obliged to provide a further argument to show why these factors would constitute good reasons for condemning it any more than we require additional arguments to show that murder is undesirable. Instead of relying exclusively on moral principles, he sought a thorough understanding of the totality of capitalist society. Presumably Marx felt that his description was damning in itself. He was also enough of a practical politician to see that capitalism could not be undermined simply by moral arguments but would require far more devastating weapons. Given this, the question of whether Marxism is prescriptive or descriptive, moralistic or scientific is misplaced. This point has been made by Wood:

> Marx's own reasons for condemning capitalism are contained in his comprehensive theory of the historical genesis, the organic functioning, and the prognosis of the capitalist mode of production. And this is not itself a *moral* theory, nor does it include any particular moral principles as such. But neither is it 'merely descriptive', in the tedious philosophical sense which is supposed to make it seem problematic how anything of that sort could ever be a reason for condemning what is so 'described'. There is nothing problematic about saying that disguised exploitation, unnecessary servitude, economic instability, and declining productivity are features of a productive system which constitute good reasons for condemning it.[24]

> No one has ever denied that capitalism, understood as Marx's theory understands it, is a system of unnecessary servitude, replete with irrationalities and ripe for destruction. Still less has anyone defended capitalism by claiming that a system of this sort might after all be good or desirable, and it is doubtful that any moral philosophy which could support such a claim would deserve serious consideration.[25]

Although Marx sees his analysis of capitalist society as an advance on that of the political economists, he does not see its superiority as resting on ethical grounds, but rather on his ability to see the various dimensions of social life as part of an historical totality.

(b) *Moral practices and modes of production*

Marx also shares with the Wittgensteinians the idea that a moral principle must be understood in terms of its social background. Phillips and Mounce refer, as we have seen, to the moral practices in terms of which ethical questions may be understood. Moral disputes are consequently seen as clashes between competing ways of life which cannot be resolved simply at a philosophical level but necessitate fundamental changes in the ways of life which generate those moral problems. Each society may contain a number of different moral practices. If we apply this analogy to Marxism, we find that Marx also treats moral, legal and juridical notions not in isolation but as intelligible only within the context of a mode of production: to be sure, the idea of a mode of production is far more extensive than a moral practice but for the purposes of our argument what is important is the fact that Marx relates principles of justice to their social setting rather than abstracting them. Once one holds a sociological view of moral life, a reliance on absolute moral principles as part of the armoury in transforming a way of life becomes untenable.

Precisely because Marx sees juridical relations as a reflection of a particular mode of production, he attaches far less importance to juridical concepts than other nineteenth-century thinkers. Until Marx's time, the juridical conception of society had been the basic property of the political philosopher who used it to examine the structure and development of society. This conception of society concentrated its analysis on the state which regulated people's actions and ascribed rights to individuals, whereas Marx rejects the centrality of the state, seeing it instead as the offshoot of a particular mode of production. All other relations in society, including legal relationships, must be seen in relation to this mode of production rather than an abstraction from it. 'This juridical relation which thus expresses itself in a contract, whether such contract be part of a developed legal system or not', says Marx, 'is a relation between two wills, and is but the reflex of the real economic relation between the two. It is this economic relation that determines the subject-matter comprised in each such juridical act'.[26]

Within the capitalist mode of production, Marxism as a mode of thought holds the uneasy position of being both generated by the mode of production and yet fundamentally opposed to it. As Marx stresses in the 'Communist manifesto', as soon as the bourgeois class rises to power it calls into being a new class which will destroy it and also the weapons it will wield against the bourgeoisie.[27] So although Marxism, as the consciousness of the proletariat, arises from the heart of the production process, this mode of thought is still fundamentally alienated from the society in so far as it expresses the ideas of the future. This idea of a plurality of different standpoints is compatible with the Wittgensteinian notion of a moral practice. Precisely because capitalist society is a class society we expect to find a number of different ideologies associated with those classes. This may seem problematic in so far as Marx's explanation of capitalist society may not be held by the majority of participants in that society whereas the Wittgensteinians, in contrast, emphasise that explanations must be couched in terms intelligible to the participants. However, as we shall see later, Winch argues that there is nothing to prevent us from using the concept of ideology provided that we relate it to the ideas possessed by members of the society.[28] Concepts such as reification, exploitation and alienation can be related to the 'common-sense' knowledge of the participants in the society.

Marx's emphasis on the mode of production should be seen as an explanatory device rather than as evidence of 'economic determinism' or of the postulation of a quasi-causal relation between economic activity and judicial and political institutions. Such institutions may be seen as *appropriate* to a particular mode of production or way of life and even necessary to its functioning. But this relationship is not a causal one: the mode of production does not *cause* itself. In this respect the virtue of Marx's notion of a totality is precisely its avoidance of a causal relationship between different institutions in society. Both modes of production and moral practices are convenient starting-points for the understanding of morality and society. Neither concept is used in a deterministic fashion but merely as a means of making social life intelligible.

(c) *Justice and injustice*

It follows from this that a mode of production should not be construed as appertaining merely to the economic sphere. As Marx says:

> The way in which men produce their means of subsistence depends first of all on the nature of the means of subsistence they actually find in existence and have to reproduce.
>
> This mode of production must not be considered simply as being the reproduction of the physical existence of the individuals. Rather it is a definite form of activity of these individuals, a definite form of expressing their life, a definite *mode of life* on their part. As individuals express their life, so they are.[29]

Central to Marx's account of the capitalist mode of production is the labour theory of value. It has often been assumed that Marx wished to establish that the workers are not paid for the full value of their labour-power and that consequently the wages they receive are unjust. Marx in fact describes the buying and selling of labour-power as 'a very Eden of the innate rights of man'. As he says:

> There alone rule Freedom, Equality, Property and Bentham. Freedom, because both buyer and seller of a commodity, say of labour-power, are constrained only by their own free will. They contract as free agents, and the agreement they come to, is but the form in which they give legal expression to their common will. Equality, because each enters into relation with the other, as with a simple owner of commodities, and they exchange equivalent for equivalent. Property, because each disposes only of what is his own. And Bentham because each looks only to himself.[30]

The worker is not only paid sufficiently but the transaction is just since the capitalist buys the commodity labour-power and pays for it at its full value. Of course by exploiting this commodity he can create surplus value but this surplus belongs to him since he now owns the commodity. Consequently he owes no one anything for the surplus and the transaction cannot be considered unjust. Indeed, to argue that every man has an unalienable right to appropriate the full value of his labour and that a denial of this right constitutes an injustice is anachronistic, for it presupposes a mode of production based on individual private property with each individual producing his own means of production, a mode of production very different from capitalism whose hallmark is the co-operation of men in the work process using the same means of production. Given that the extraction of surplus value is the fundamental and defining feature of capitalism, there can be no moral objection to this practice *within* the framework of the capitalist mode of production. Moral objections are precisely what Marx avoids:

> The seller of labour-power, like the seller of any other commodity, realises its exchange-value, and parts with its use-value. He cannot take the one without giving the other. The use-value of labour-power or in other words, labour, belongs just as little to its seller, as the use-value of oil after it has been sold belongs to the dealer who has sold it. The owner of the money has paid the value of a day's labour-power; his, therefore, is the use of it for a day; a day's labour belongs to him. The circumstance, that on the one hand the daily sustenance of labour-power costs only half a day's labour, while on the other hand the very same labour-power can work during a whole day, that consequently the value which its use during one day creates, is double what he pays for that use, this circumstance is, without doubt, a piece of good luck for the buyer, but by no means an injury to the seller.[31]

In this sense the extraction of surplus value is just and to deprive the capitalist of it would be unjust since it is not an abuse of capitalist production nor an unfair practice within capitalism but rather constitutes its essence and therefore cannot be removed by social and political reforms. Only a fundamental change in the mode of production could achieve this and for Marx this would not arise from the weight of moral arguments against capitalism but through the breakdown of the society brought about by its fundamental irrationalities and contradictions.

It is perhaps not surprising that Marx rejected the application of notions of justice and injustice to capitalist social relations since he had little confidence that exploitation might be removed by the demand for an extension of human rights. Like Hegel, he was suspicious of the abstract ideals of the French Revolution which he thought would serve to divert the working class away from its historical role as the agent of social change and ultimately served to mask particular interests, as he observes in 'On the Jewish Question':

> None of the so-called rights of man, therefore, go beyond egoistic man, beyond man as a member of civil society, that is, an individual withdrawn into himself, into the confines of his private interests and private caprice, and separated from the community. In the rights of man, he is far from being conceived as a species-being; on the contrary, species-life itself, society, appears as a framework external to the individuals, as a restriction of their original independence. The sole bond holding them together is natural necessity, need and private interest, the preservation of their property and their egoistic selves.[32]

The conceptions of liberty and equality in the Declaration of the Rights of Man reduced the individual to a 'self-sufficient monad'[33] governed by self-interest. The particularism inherent in these 'universal rights' soon revealed itself:

> Finally, in 1830 the bourgeoisie put into effect its wishes of the year 1789, with the only difference that its *political enlightenment* was now *completed,* that it no longer considered the constitutional representative state as a means for achieving the ideal of the state, the welfare of the world and universal human aims but, on the contrary, had acknowledged it as the *official* expression of its own *exclusive* power and the *political* recognition of its own *special* interests.[34]

But if the extraction of surplus value cannot be criticised by an appeal to justice or human rights but, as we have seen, can be defended as just, then why did Marx offer a critique of capitalism? This question is considered by Wood who tries to rescue Marx from charges of moralism. He rightly argues that juridical principles cannot be used as the basis for a critique of capitalism, and hence, as a point of comparison with communism since 'Marx holds that "juridical relations" (*Rechtsverhältnisse*), matters involving rights or justice, all "arise out of economic relations", and constitute no sort of Archimedean point outside, or foundation beneath these relations on the basis of which they might be criticised'.[35] Instead Wood offers a possible point of comparison in terms of what he describes as non-moral goods, in contrast to the moral goods favoured by those who attribute a moral theory to Marx. Non-moral goods embrace pleasure and happiness as well as self-actualisation while 'moral goods' would include justice, right and virtue, all of which are missing from Marx's critique of capitalism for,

> Marx bases his critique of capitalism on the claim that it frustrates many important *non-moral* goods: self-actualization, security, physical health, comfort, community, freedom. Of course the distinction between moral and non-moral goods is never explicitly drawn by Marx, but it is a familiar one (both in philosophy and in everyday life) and it is not implausible to think Marx might be tacitly aware of it and even make significant use of it without consciously attending to it.[36]

It is on this basis, he argues, that Marx constructs his critique of capitalism and counterposes a communist society which can deliver these non-moral goods. However, there are a number of difficulties with this distinction. To begin with, can moral goods and non-moral goods be so easily separated? As Arneson has noted, questions of fairness of distribution could be said to arise on both sides of the distinction and maldistribution, he argues, is central to Marx's critique.[37] Certainly, the non-moral goods he cites seem to correspond to the 'primary goods' utilised in Rawls's theory of justice.[38] Confusion could also arise from Wood's conflation of comfort and self-actualisation within the category of non-moral goods, particularly as he also argues that the quest for self-actualisation may engender discomfort. By placing the two items within the same category, he is also in danger of falling into a crude utilitarian position. Although critical of utilitarianism, Wood does describe capitalism as serving 'the interests and needs of fewer and fewer' and calculates that the social changes associated with capitalism 'had taken away from human happiness perhaps more than was added by the increase in human productive capacities'.[39] Furthermore, while he rightly rejects communism as an 'ideal', citing instead Marx's remark in the *Grundrisse* that it 'is an actual movement which is abolishing the present state of affairs', he none the less sees communism as superior to capitalism in so far as it can provide for the non-moral goods. So while Wood rightly rules out the use of justice as a point of comparison, he offers instead another comparative principle, namely self-actualisation, whereas Marx excludes external principles. The difficulty of establishing an external principle is borne out by the fact the goods identified by Wood are very much cultural products and their externality is illusory. If we contrast the hedonism of nineteenth-century utilitarians and twentieth-century Marxists with the asceticism of seventeenth-century Protestants, we can see the degree to which modern commentators remain trapped within the modes of thought of their age. While providing a plausible critique of moralistic interpretations of Marxism, Wood ironically takes up a similar position to Taylor in ultimately seeing communism as *better* on the grounds that it provides greater opportunities for fulfilment as well as happiness and comfort.

In the absence of external moral standards against which different societies can be measured, the communist society described by Marx cannot be viewed as a 'morally superior' alternative. Consequently Marx cannot be seen as advancing a moral theory. On the contrary he argues in the 'Critique of the Gotha programme' that 'Right can never be higher than the economic structure of society and the cultural development conditioned by it'.[40] Communism, as a new mode of production, will therefore give rise to its own peculiar judicial and moral institutions and practices appropriate to that way of life.

But in denying the superior *ethical* status of communism, Marx does not rule out its superiority on other grounds. One might, for example, contrast the irrationality of capitalism with the rationality of communism.[41] In condemning capitalism and pointing to its defects Marx's starting-point is the structure and development of capitalism rather than an appeal to human rights or the felicific calculus. Thus he offers an evolutionary model of social development in so far as he sees society as passing through a number of distinct stages, each characterised by a distinctive set of social relationships arising from the specific mode of production. Each represents a more advanced stage of development of the productive forces and in this sense is superior to its predecessors. Hence in commenting on the Russo-Turkish war of 1877, Marx expresses his admiration for the 'gallant Turks'.[42] He regards them as superior to the Russians precisely because in defeating them, they were speeding up the possibility of revolution in Europe. In a letter to Sorge he describes the war as 'a new turning-*point* in European history ... This time the revolution begins in the East, hitherto the unbroken bulwark and reserve army of counter-revolution'.[43] Here we can note that Marx's principle of evaluation is *internal* to the society rather than resting on an abstract moral principle. In this sense we might say that capitalism is perceived and experienced as unjust from the standpoint of the working class only in so far as they represent the new developing forces of production.

But in excluding such principles from our evaluation, are we then in danger of reducing Marxism to a relativist position? This objection is hard to sustain, for if we dismiss Marx as a relativist simply because he insists that the justice of an institution depends on its social context, then we condemn all social science to relativism. Moreover, to say that each institution must be understood in its social context does not rule out the possibility of definite lines of continuity between different historical periods. Indeed Marx, like Hegel, speaks of domination and servitude as characteristic of all modes of production in human history up to the present. Continuity is also expressed in Roman law, a point stressed by Lefebvre:

> Marx and Engels put great emphasis on the importance of Roman law. It has persisted – not without modifications and adjustments – through a number of modes of production, a number of societies (slavery, feudalism, capitalism, and even socialism), thus showing that it cannot be classified as a mere 'superstructure' or institution. As a form of human relations it has a foundation deeper and more lasting than production relations. It regulates interindividual and intergroup relations so long as the products of social labour are not sufficiently abundant to be distributed evenly. Legal justice is the corollary of injustice. *Summum ius, summa iniuria.* Be that as it may, juridical form is not isolated from the other basic forms, which have been imposed upon human contents, products, works, activities – formal logic, the commodity form, the forms of language and discourse.[44]

This code governs the relationships between people and the state and helps us to understand society by giving a coherent form to contractual relations. While the codes in different societies are not identical, they do share certain common principles. Hence, in socialist societies we still have contracts and legal rights. However, Lefebvre points out that in a truly communist society the possibility of transcending the code emerges:

> Only a communist society, a society of plenty governed by the maxim 'To each according to his needs, from each according to his capacities', will be able to dispense with a formal body of laws, norms, formal maxims, and gradually, in unforeseen ways, go back to the rule of custom. Until this historical moment has been reached, juridical sociology, the formalised sociological study of institutions, will remain an especially important aspect of the study of class relations, i.e. of a properly Marxian sociology.[45]

If there is a possibility that Roman law may be superseded in the future, could morality also be superseded?

Morality in communist society

Considerable attention has been paid within Marxism, to the question of the morality of future communist society and we can identify two major strands of thought: the first sees communist society as the supremely moral society in so far as it is able to provide the ethical life lacking in capitalism, while the second argues for an elimination of morality. The former follows logically from arguments for a Marxist morality. Taylor and Gould, for example, as we noted earlier, establish the supremacy of communism on ethical grounds, namely that it is able to provide for a full self-realisation of human beings and therefore embodies the principles of freedom and justice.[46] At the other extreme, Marxists, equating morality with ideology, have seen the attack on morality as an essential feature of Marxism and have emphasised the need to transcend it in communism. If Marx does treat juridical, religious and moral beliefs as ideological, it would seem to follow that morality can and should disappear in communist society. Skillen, for example, colourfully describes morality as 'the missionary advance party of capitalism's divide and rule attack' and argues for a 'radical-materialist' alternative.[47] This point is taken up by Collier who argues for an end to morality in communist society and its replacement by 'practical reason' which would involve the satisfaction of needs rather than the application of ethical principles.[48] By satisfaction of needs, he seems to be referring to the 'non-moral goods' cited by Wood, namely pleasure and happiness as opposed to right and justice. 'What must be decisively rejected', he argues,' is any attempt to inculcate a "higher socialist morality", whether this is the old bourgeois morality writ large, as in state-capitalist countries, or some new ideal worked out in abstraction from real human needs'.[49]

Both these solutions to the question raise problems. The first approach, as we have already argued, cannot be reconciled with Marx's rejection of abstract principles and his grounding of morality within particular modes of production. The second approach, while *prima facie* more attractive since it recognises Marx's contempt for moralising and moralisers, cannot be sustained. By arguing for an 'end to morality', the proponents of the latter view misconstrue Marx's critique of bourgeois morality and in effect confuse *bourgeois* morality with morality *per se*. For Marx saw morality as an essential part of sociality, as we can see from the following remarks:

> But the *community* from which the worker is *isolated* is a community the real character and scope of which is quite different from that of the *political* community. The community from which the worker is isolated by *his own labour* is *life* itself, physical and mental life, human morality, human activity, human enjoyment, *human* nature. *Human nature* is the *true community* of men.[50]

One can be too easily misled by Marx's vitriolic attack on bourgeois morality into underestimating the role morality plays in social life and to reduce morality to mere legitimations. All social groups encounter moral problems in transforming the world and will see certain courses of action as morally superior to others. Morality, in this sense, is an essential dimension of culture. Which ends will be valued in the society of the future is, of course, difficult to predict and Marx rightly steers clear of such prophecies. Changes in the way of life of a society may eliminate certain moral problems, but as Wittgenstein has argued, this will not necessarily mean an end to all such problems:

> The sickness of a time is cured by an alteration in the mode of life of human beings, and it was possible for the sickness of philosophical problems to get cured only through a changed mode of thought and of life, not through a medicine invented by an individual.
>
> Suppose the use of the motor-car produces or encourages certain illnesses, and mankind is plagued by such illness until, from some cause or other, as the result of some development or other, it abandons the habit of driving.[51]

Of course the nature of morality will change with the emergence of a new mode of production, as class-conditioned moralities disappear with the classes who uphold them and as new technologies emerge to shape the new social structure. The moral obligations of a Victorian family firm, for example, are no longer relevant to a mode of production dominated by multinational companies. Social and technological changes may solve specific problems but cannot be seen as leading to a destruction or elimination of morality: instead, one set of moral problems is exchanged for another. Acknowledgement of the persistence of morality by Marx and Wittgenstein constitutes an acceptance of its importance in social life. At the same time they recognise that *particular* moral problems depend on a certain level of cultural and technological development and that these problems therefore cannot be solved by an appeal to individual conscience and decision nor ethical principles, but rather only through cultural and technological transformations. Given this, the alternative to morality proposed by Collier *et al.*, in which the individual pursues his own particular ends, seems parasitic on the 'psychologism' of contemporary society, itself rooted in individualism.[52] At the same time, in postulating a conception of 'real human needs', albeit a conception distinct from that of Taylor and Gould, Collier seems to be in danger of adopting a transcendentalist position. Moreover, in reducing morality to mere legitimations, he overlooks the meaning that values such as honesty and truth-telling can have within a particular form of life. So while Collier's conception of Marxism as an *alternative* to morality is understandable in the light of Marx's rejection of bourgeois morality, it cannot be supported for the reasons given above.

Marx seeks to avoid both these extreme positions by giving a sociological account of morality. He demonstrates that description and evaluation cannot be separated and that juridical conceptions must be understood in relation to the mode of production in which they arise. In the absence of an absolute notion of justice, it is mistaken to see Marx as offering a critique of capitalism based simply on moral principles. Rather, his critique of capitalism is contained within his account of the capitalist mode of production. Whilst this critique is not reducible to a moral theory, it does incorporate evaluative elements in so far as Marx's description also amounts to a condemnation of capitalist society. We might say that Marx examines the facts evaluatively while also considering values from a 'factual', objective, historical standpoint, and in this sense he transcends the fact–value distinction. In Marx's work description and evaluation cannot be meaningfully separated since he is committed neither to positivism nor to an ethical theory but instead tries to overcome the fact–value distinction in his account of the practices of capitalist society. His account takes as its starting-point the process of production and the institutions of capitalist society, but in discovering its weaknesses and contradictions, he is committed to its abolition.

Communism, for Marx, is superior in so far as it deals with the problems generated by the irrational nature of capitalist society and is able to develop the productive forces. But this superiority does not amount to *ethical* superiority. In portraying communist society in this light, Marx considers the possibility of an alternative way of life with its own moral and judicial standards. Indeed, the fact that Marx did not provide blueprints for future communist society is itself symptomatic of his awareness of the difficulties involved in the attempt to describe in detail a form of life based on principles different from our own.

Given this, we should see Marxism as akin to a world-view with its own standards rather than as a moral theory. Different world-views may therefore be seen as incommensurable, with adherents to the different views being unable to discuss their differences in a rational way since their basic premises are so far apart. Moving from one world-view to another involves a change both in ideas and activities since a world-view is grounded in a particular form of life. We will therefore now examine more thoroughly what is involved in the notion of a world-view and some of the difficulties raised by this notion.

Notes to Chapter III

[1] This chapter incorporates a revised version of a paper 'Facts, values and Marxism', published in *Studies in Soviet Thought* (1977).

[2] M. Weber, *The Methodology of the Social Sciences*, trans. Shils and Finch (Glencoe: Free Press, 1949).

[3] For a discussion of this approach, see J. Habermas, 'Dogmatism, reason and decision: on theory and praxis in our scientific civilization', *Theory and Practice*, pp. 243–82.

[4] G. A. Cohen, 'Karl Marx and the withering away of social science', *Philosophy and Public Affairs* II (1972), pp. 182–203.

[5] F. Engels, 'The condition of the working class in England', *Collected Works* IV; *Socialism: Utopian and Scientific* (Moscow: Progress Publishers, 1968).

[6] F. Engels, *Socialism: Utopian and Scientific*, p. 50.

[7] *Ibid*., p. 70.

[8] J. Hoffman, *Marxism and the Theory of Praxis*: 'For it is a dangerous and sectarian blunder to imagine that workers' councils, which represent all the workers at a point of production, are a *substitute* for the leading role of a Communist Party and its political allies which must tackle the problems of planning the society *as a whole*. The real and complex problems of constructing socialist forms of production in town and countryside on the basis of the capitalist society of the past will assuredly not be solved by the cry for "workers' control", and in fact as Lukács's own Hungary showed so tragically in the counter-revolution of 1956, it is by no means impossible for "workers councils" to be demagogically used as an *attack* on the institutions of socialism. A sobering thought' (p. 230).

[9] K. Popper, *The Open Society; The Poverty of Historicism* (London: Routledge and Kegan Paul, 1957); *Conjectures and Refutations* (London: Routledge and Kegan Paul, 1963).

[10] K. Popper, *Conjectures and Refutations*, p. 37. However, the use of falsifiability as a criterion of demarcation between science and non-science has been criticised by a number of philosophers of science, including J. Krige, who argues that falsifiability is in fact prohibitive of new developments rather than a means of ensuring free scientific inquiry, *Science, Revolution and Discontinuity* (Brighton: Harvester Press, 1980); for discussion of testability in relation to Marxism, see G. Lukács, 'What is orthodox Marxism', *History and Class Consciousness* (London: Merlin Press, 1971) pp. 1–26; T. B. Bottomore, 'Class structure and social consciousness', *Sociology and Social Criticism* (London: Allen and Unwin, 1975); H. Marcuse, 'Karl Popper and the problem of historical laws', *Studies in Critical Philosophy* (London: New Left Books, 1972).

[11] C. Taylor, 'Marxism and empiricism', *British Analytical Philosophy*, ed. B. Williams and A. Montefiore (London: Routledge and Kegan Paul, 1966); see also E. Kamenka, *The Ethical Foundations of Marxism* (London: Routledge and Kegan Paul, 1962).

[12] C. Taylor, *op. cit*., pp. 244–5.

[13] C. Gould, *Marx's Social Ontology*.

[14] P. T. Geach, 'Good and evil', *Analysis* XVII, No. 2; G. E. M. Anscombe, 'Moral philosophy', *Philosophy* XXXIII (Jan. 1958); P. Foot, 'When is a principle a moral principle?', *Aristotelian Society Proceedings*, XXVIII (1954); 'Moral Beliefs', *Aristotelian Society Proceedings* (1958); 'Moral Arguments', *Mind* (1958); 'Goodness and Choice', *Aristotelian Society Proceedings*, XXXV (1961).

[15] D. P. H. Allen, 'Is Marxism a philosophy?', *Journal of Philosophy*, LXXI (1974), pp. 601–12.

[16] K. Marx, *Capital* I, p. 609.

[17] K. Marx, *Grundrisse*.

[18] K. Marx and F. Engels, 'The German ideology', p. 53.

[19] P. Winch, 'Understanding a primitive society', *Ethics and Action* (London: Routledge and Kegan Paul, 1972).

[20] D. Z. Phillips, 'Does it pay to be good?', *Aristotelian Society Proceedings*, LXV (1964–5); D. Z. Phillips and H. O. Mounce, 'On morality's having a point', *Philosophy* (Oct. 1965); these articles are developed in D. Z. Phillips and H. O. Mounce, *Moral Practices* (London: Routledge and Kegan Paul, 1969).

[21] Of course, one can lie on certain occasions with a clear conscience as, for example, when one tells white lies. A doctor who refuses to tell his patient that he is dying, thereby lying about his health, would be one example. But because lying is generally wrong one has to provide justifications and virtuous reasons to cover the occasions when one knowingly lies. Truth telling does not require such an additional justification. Apart from those occasions where reasons are supplied, there is no logical gulf between determining that a man has lied and concluding that he has done wrong.

[22] R. M. Hare, *The Language of Morals* (Oxford: University Press, 1962); P. Foot, *op. cit.*

[23] R. J. Arneson, 'What's wrong with exploitation?', *Ethics* (Jan. 1981).

[24] A. Wood, 'The Marxian critique of justice', *Philosophy and Public Affairs* I, 3, (spring 1972) pp. 281–2.

[25] *Ibid.*, p. 282.

[26] K. Marx, *Capital* I, p. 84.

[27] K. Marx and F. Engels, 'Manifesto of the Communist Party', *Collected Works* VI, p. 490.

[28] P. Winch, unpublished 'Notes for joint session' (Swansea, 1967).

[29] K. Marx and F. Engels, 'The German ideology', *Collected Works* V, p. 31.

[30] K. Marx, *Capital* I, p. 176.

[31] *Ibid.*, p. 193.

[32] K. Marx, 'On the Jewish question', *Collected Works* III, p. 164.

[33] *Ibid.*, p. 163.

[34] K. Marx and F. Engels, 'The Holy Family', *Collected Works* IV, p. 124.

[35] A. Wood, *Karl Marx* (London: Routledge and Kegan Paul, 1981) p. 43.

[36] *Ibid.*, p. 127.

[37] R. J. Arneson, *op. cit.*

[38] J. Rawls, *A Theory of Justice* (Oxford: Clarendon Press, 1972).

[39] A. Wood, 'The Marxian critique of justice', *Philosophy and Public Affairs* I, 3, (spring 1972), p. 275.

[40] K. Marx, 'Critique of the Gotha programme', *Marx and Engels: Basic Writings in Politics and Philosophy* ed. L. S. Feuer (London: Pelican, 1963) p. 160.

[41] See J. Habermas, *Towards a Rational Society* (London: Heinemann, 1971); *Legitimation Crisis* (London: Heinemann, 1976).

[42] K. Marx, letter to Sorge, 27 Sept. 1877, *Selected Correspondence* (Moscow, 1956).

[43] *Ibid.*: Marx is here making a similar point to Saint-Simon, who had earlier criticised Thierry's history of the Norman conquest of England because it gave too much emphasis to the racial conflict generated by the conquest rather than concentrating on the social progress it had generated. This, for Saint-Simon, was the only possible criterion for historical judgement.

[44] H. Lefebvre, *The Sociology of Marx* (London: Penguin, 1972), pp. 113–4.

[45] *Ibid.*, p. 115.

[46] C. Taylor, *op. cit.*; C. Gould, *op. cit.*

[47] T. Skillen, 'Marxism and morality', *Radical Philosophy* VIII (summer 1974) p. 14.

[48] A. Collier, 'The production of moral ideology', *Radical Philosophy* IX (winter 1974) pp. 5–15.

[49] *Ibid.*, p. 13.

[50] K. Marx, 'Marginal notes on the article by a Prussian', *Collected Works* III, p. 204.

[51] L. Wittgenstein, *Remarks on the Foundations of Mathematics* (Oxford: Basil Blackwell, 1967), p. 57e.

[52] P. Berger, 'Towards a sociological understanding of psycho-analysis', *Social Research* XXXII (1965), pp. 26–41.

IV

World-visions and world-pictures

In this chapter we will compare the Marxian notion of a world-view or world-vision with the Wittgensteinian concept of a world-picture. Although the notion of a world-view has a long history within Hegelian Marxism, we will focus specifically on its use by Goldmann, who applies Marx's insights into the relationship between ideas and social life specifically to the realm of literature.[1] Although Goldmann and Wittgenstein are dealing with different subject-areas, they none the less share much common ground. Both stress the totality rather than the individual as the focus of literary production and cognition respectively. Both see ideas, thoughts and activities as conducted within a framework which, although philosophical, is internally related to that way of life. Hence a world-vision expresses the life-experiences of the class in so far as membership of the class determines the limits of consciousness for its members. A similar awareness of the 'limits of thought' is encapsulated in the idea of a world-picture advanced by Wittgenstein in *On Certainty*.[2] This notion can therefore throw light on problems raised within the Marxian tradition concerning the relationship between being and consciousness and the nature of ideology. At the same time both Marx and Wittgenstein reject crude mechanistic notions of the relationship between base and superstructure.

By elucidating the notion of a world-vision, we hope to bypass some of the problems which arise when construing ideologies or 'false consciousness' in terms of the essence–appearance distinction. Ironically, the idea of a world-view has come under attack from within Marxism for failing to give a full account of social life because it emphasises the properties of the individual rather than the class.[3] Yet, as we have seen, it is the essence–appearance account of ideology rather than the notion of a world-view which rests on the individual as the basis of cognition.

The categories, ideas and assumptions which compose the world-view can only be examined within the context of the social conditions in which they flourish. This notion may be contrasted with theories of ideology which employ empiricist models of the misperception and sensory delusion of the abstract individual. It also provides a further starting-point for a consideration of the common ground shared by Marx and Wittgenstein.

Abstraction and totality

The idea of an abstract individual with needs, wants and desires that remain static regardless of changing historical circumstances is anathema to Marx, for whom society is not reducible to individuals,but rather 'expresses the sum of interrelations, the relations within which these individuals stand'.[4] He sees the fascination with the abstract individual as characteristic of the classical economists:

> Even the best spokesmen of classical economy remain more or less in the grip of the world of illusion which their criticism had dissolved, as cannot be otherwise from a bourgeois standpoint, and thus they all fall more or less into inconsistencies, half-truths and unsolved contradictions.[5]

Marx traces the development of the abstract individual in the *Grundrisse* where he notes that looking back into the past the individual is inseparable from the social whole, 'in a still quite natural way in the family and in the family expanded into the clan, then later in the various forms of communal society arising out of the antitheses and fusions of the clans',[6] but with the rise of bourgeois society, characterised by free competition, individuation develops. Although this society has 'the most highly developed social relations' in so far as the individual can individuate himself only in the social milieu, nonetheless, in such a privatised society the illusion of the abstract individual flourishes: 'the individual appears detached from the natural bonds etc. which in earlier historical periods make him the accessory of a definite and limited human conglomerate'.[7] Marx's contemporaries used the model of the abstract individual 'not as a historic result but as history's point of departure', projecting it back into the past and forward into the future, thereby precluding alternative conceptions of social life.[8] Against this, Marx argues that it does not make sense to talk of an individual existing, that is, producing, apart from society:

> Production by an isolated individual outside society – a rare exception which may well occur when a civilized person in whom the social forces are already dynamically present is cast by accident into the wilderness – is as much of an absurdity as is the development of language without individuals living *together* and talking to each other.[9]
>
> All production is appropriation of nature on the part of an individual within and through a specific form of society.[10]
>
> Whenever we speak of production, then, what is meant is always production at a definite stage of social development – production by social individuals.[11]

The same point has been made by Bukharin who contrasts 'the practice of social man, transforming the objective world', with the individual 'practice' of the 'philistine in a beershop':[12]

> And so man is historically given as *social* man (in contradistinction to the enlightened Robinsons of *Rousseau*, 'founding' society and history like a chess club, and with the help of a 'contract'. This social man, i.e. human society, in order to live, *must produce. Am Anfang war die Tat* (in contrast to the Christian Logos: "In the beginning was the Word"). Production is the real starting point of social development. In the process of production there takes place a 'metabolism' (Marx) between society and nature. In this process, *active* on the part of historical and social man, a *material* process, people are in definite relationship one with another and with the means of labour.[13]

Like Marx, Wittgenstein saw individual action as necessarily social action: men are still social beings even when they work as individuals, in so far as they share a system of ideas. Similarly, Winch argues that the debate between methodological individualists and holists is misguided since it relies on a false distinction between social phenomena and individual behaviour.[14]

Echoing Bukharin, Wittgenstein refers to Goethe's '... und schreib getrost "Im Anfang war die Tat"!'.[15] The production of language, like commodities, is explicable only in the context of publicly-shared meanings. Just as language is more than an aggregate of symbols, so an industrial society is more than aggregate of individual producers and consumers. Like Marx, he sees the possibility of language without social interaction as absurd:

> It would be possible to imagine people who had something not quite unlike a language: a play of sounds, without vocabulary or grammar, ('Speaking with tongues').[16]
>
> 'But what would the meaning of the sounds be in such a case?' – What is it in music? Though I don't at all wish to say that this language of a play of sounds would have to be compared to music.[17]

In stressing that the relations of production of society form a whole, Marx does not offer a crude organic analogy of the kind favoured by Spencer and the functionalists but instead emphasises the historical nature of this organic totality which is characterised by the dynamic tension between classes.[18] This also has implications for the Marxist model of revolution. If society is organically constructed yet constantly in a state of flux, it follows that even minor changes have far-reaching implications. This seems to challenge the traditional dichotomy between revolutionary and evolutionary development. A synthesis of the two extremes is suggested by the concept of 'revolutionary reformism', cited by Goldmann, who argues that in the post-1968 period, the dichotomy has been transcended:

> precisely because of all the phenomena of this year, of which the most important have been those of the Spring in Czechoslovakia and in France, it marks one of the most important turning points in the history of industrial societies and of the contemporary world. It is in relation to this turning point that the old words 'reform', 'revolution', 'socialism', 'capitalism', 'liberalism', 'democracy', change their meaning and will only remain valid to the extent to which one gives them a new meaning ... The most important terms of socialist theoretical thought change their content and their nature: 'reform', which was the opposite of 'revolution', and signified adaption to the existing system, becomes the first stage of the revolution, the road to the transformation of the system, and the principal current of modern socialism calls itself, in the West, revolutionary reformism.[19]

While not calling explicitly for a total transformation of society, forms of social struggle characterised by a piecemeal reformist nature can have extensive repercussions. Although limited in their objectives, the anti-Vietnam war movement, the French and Italian workers who went on strike in 1968 and 1969, the 'flying pickets' of 1972 have *all* had far-reaching effects, the extent of which has yet to be calculated. To these struggles, exhibiting the character of revolutionary reformism:

> The traditional schema of socialist thought: first, politics and the conquest of the state; then, social and economic transformations is being replaced by an inverse schema: transformations of the social and economic structure of immediate life (factory, university, commune, etc.) leading in the end to a transformation of the political structures and of the state.[20]

The kinds of changes which Goldmann sees as 'revolutionary–reformist' are not merely piecemeal changes but represent a global or universal alternative, namely, a democratic society characterised by full participation in decision-making processes, in contrast to both the socialism of the East and Western capitalism. In revolutionary reformist demands, universal objectives are reflected in particular forms: for example, an occupation of a specific factory over, say, better working conditions, can reflect a universal demand for the humanisation of labour. These reformist demands made within the system at the same time reflect universal values incompatible with that system and thus generate tensions within the society. The distinction between the particular and the universal, like so many of the dichotomies erected by empiricism, is thus transcended in Marxism. For the nature of contemporary political struggles and their reflection in Goldmann's Marxism calls into question the distinction between piecemeal and holistic social change.

The category of totality determines both the subject and object of knowledge. The object, namely class society, must be studied as a whole but it can be grasped only if the subject which grasps it is itself a totality, that is, a class. Hence, Marxism studies capitalist society from the standpoint of the working class, bringing to light problems which would not be noticed by those who study it from the standpoint of the individual. For Marx there are no absolute individuals or absolute wholes: being mutually definable, they are dependent on each other. The dialectical relationship between individual and society is explained by neither the objective structures nor the attitudes of an individual but by the relationship between them. He seeks to transcend the false dichotomy between the individual and society, stressing that neither should be abstracted or reified:

> Above all we must avoid postulating 'society' again as an abstraction *vis-à-vis* the individual. The individual *is the social being*. His manifestations of life – even if they may not appear in the direct form of *communal* manifestations of life carried out in association with others – *are* therefore an expression and confirmation of *social life*. Man's individual and species-life are not *different*, however much – and this is inevitable – the mode of existence of the individual is a more *particular* or more *general* mode of the life of the species, or the life of the species is a more *particular* or more *general* individual life.[21]

This has been emphasised by Gould who notes that 'for Marx ... the primary ontological subject is, properly speaking, a social individual'.[22] Sociality is the essential feature of the mode of life of individuals and social relations cannot be understood apart from individuals, 'thus these individuals have fundamental ontological status and are not to be understood as mere nodes of relations or as wholly constituted by their relations'.[23]

The notions of abstraction and totality have been developed by Lukács, who argues that because 'bourgeois thought' is abstracted it arrives at a one-sided picture of social life and is therefore ideological. However, in attacking abstract thought, Lukács formulates a distinction between legitimate and illegitimate abstraction:

> Marxism, however, simultaneously raises and reduces all specialisations to the level of aspects in a dialectical process. This is not to deny that the process of abstraction and hence the isolation of the elements and concepts in the special disciplines and whole areas of study is of the very essence of science. But what is decisive is whether this process of isolation is a means towards understanding the whole and whether it is integrated within the context it presupposes and requires, or whether the abstract knowledge of an isolated fragment retains its 'autonomy' and becomes an end in itself. In the last analysis Marxism does not acknowledge the existence of independent sciences of law, economics or history, etc: there is nothing but a single, unified – dialectical and historical – science of the evolution of society as a totality.[24]

While abstraction has a role to play in science, the abstracted elements need to be reinserted into a totality. So essential is the category of totality that Lukács, in his essay 'What is orthodox Marxism?', defines Marxism in terms of its use of the category of totality, its attempt to grasp history as a unified process by recognising the systematic and necessary connections between different events, in terms of the relationships of domination and servitude at each stage of development of the productive forces, and its analysis of the totality of social relationships from the standpoint of the totality, that is, the class rather than the individual.[25]

Goldmann: world-visions

Goldmann draws heavily on Lukács's concept of totality in developing his notion of a world-vision. For Goldmann, great works of literature and philosophy constitute an expression of the world-vision of a particular group or class. He describes a world-vision as follows:

> What I have called a 'world vision' is a convenient term for the whole complex of ideas, aspirations and feelings which links together the members of a social group (a group which, in most cases, assumes the existence of a social class) and which opposes them to members of other social groups. This is ... a tendency which really exists among the members of a certain social group, who all attain this class consciousness in a more or less coherent manner ... In a few cases – and it is these which interest us – there are exceptional individuals who actually achieve or who come very near to achieving a completely integrated and coherent view of what they and the social class to which they belong are trying to do. The men who express this vision on an imaginative or conceptual plane are writers and philosophers, and the more closely their work expresses this vision in its complete and integrated form, the more important does it become. They then achieve the maximum possible awareness of the social group whose nature they are expressing.[26]

A world-vision may be understood as a total understanding of the world which tries to grasp its meaning in all its diversity and unity. All great literary works, according to Goldmann, express world-visions, which are the theoretical expressions of the life-experiences and interests of particular social classes and constitute a collective consciousness which unites members of the class.

Classes thus provide the infrastructure of world-visions and provide a medium through which the writer is linked to the decisive social and political events of his time. No articulate member of a class can be indifferent to such events. On the contrary his class affiliations sharpen his consciousness of the world and drive him to express the more significant social tendencies of the period in a literary or philosophical form. But, for Goldmann, not all groups based on economic interests constitute classes; it is only when their interests are directed towards a complete transformation of the social structure or towards maintaining the present social structure unchanged that they may be properly described as classes.[27] Each class will then express this desire for change or permanence in a complete vision of how social life should be organised.

One of the advantages of historical materialism, says Goldmann, is its ability to study intellectual and artistic phenomena as expressions of a collective consciousness. It therefore needs no recourse to metaphysical or psychological hypotheses. The notion of a world-vision as a collective consciousness does not, however, simply imply an arithmetical sum of autonomous and independent entities any more than Rousseau's *Volonté générale* can be understood as the will of fifty million Frenchmen.[28] Goldmann argues that class consciousness is the totality of states of individual consciousness and of other tendencies, resulting from their mutual influence upon one another and from their relationship to nature. Each component can only be understood in terms of the totality of its relations with other components rather than as an individual unity. In this sense the concept of totality Goldmann borrows from Lukács is that of a dynamic organic totality rather than a mere aggregate.

The structure of the work of the individual artist cannot be seen as his own personal property but rather as an expression of the consciousness of the social group to which he belongs. An individual artist is limited by his class membership, for the totality of social relations between individuals gives rise to the continual formation of certain 'psychic structures' common to individuals who are members of the same class. By 'psychic structures', Goldmann means a coherent perspective which sets limits to awareness. Here he is reiterating Marx's point in the *Eighteenth Brumaire* that the intellectual representatives of a class do not transcend at an ideological level the material existence of the class:

> Just as little must one imagine that the democratic representatives are indeed all shopkeepers or enthusiastic champions of shopkeepers. According to their education and their individual position they may be as far apart as heaven from earth. What makes them representatives of the petty bourgeoisie is the fact that in their minds they do not get beyond the limits which the latter do not get beyond in life, that they are consequently driven, theoretically, to the same problems and solutions to which material interest and social position drive the latter practically. This is, in general, the relationship between the *political* and *literary representatives* of a class and the class they represent.[29]

For Marx, the person who views the world from the standpoint of the individual capitalist is unable to arrive at a complete picture of social life, and in this sense his thought is ideological. These limits can be construed in relation to his activities within capitalist society, his life-style and the ideas related to those activities. To transcend these limits he must change his way of life as well as his ideas.[30]

In developing Marx's notion of the limits of consciousness, Goldmann refers to the plays of Racine and considers whether the relationship between Racine's plays and his social background is contingent or necessary. At one level, says Goldmann, the relationship is contingent:

> ... if the young Racine, as can easily be conceived, had been brought up, not in a Jansenist milieu, but, let us say, among the Jesuits, he would certainly not have written the *same* plays. He would have written different plays, implying a different vision of man and of the world. We can see that, on the biographical plane of the relation to the *individual* subject, Racine's dramas appear connected to an accident: the author's education at Port-Royal. Therefore, neither the structure nor the genesis of his dramas present a necessary character.[31]

But the connection is a necessary one in the sense that whoever had written the plays expressing the aspirations of the class, the *Noblesse de Robe* and the persecuted religious group, the Jansenists, these plays would embody what Goldmann calls a tragic vision:

> By referring to the social group which elaborated the tragic vision in 17th-century France, that is, the Noblesse de Robe, and to the Jansenist movement, it becomes clear that while Racine's tragedies might not have been written if there had been no writer of genius capable of giving literary expression to the possible consciousness of the group, it was certainly inconceivable that this group should as a transindividual subject, have given rise to an Epicurean and mystical literary expression. In this sense, the connection between Racine's tragedies and Jansenism, and the Noblesse de Robe, is *necessary* in a way that the connections between them and the writer himself are not.[32]

But if the writer expresses the limits of consciousness of his class, what are the possibilities of him engaging in work of a truly original nature? Goldmann deals with this problem by arguing that a world-vision is *implicit* in the beliefs and practices of day-to-day life but is expressed and clarified in artistic and philosophical works. Hence, in *The Human Sciences and Philosophy* he points out that the sociologist of knowledge may study world-visions on two different planes: firstly in terms of the *real* consciousness of the group or class and secondly in terms of the *potential* consciousness.[33] The former refers to the consciousness expressed by the class in everyday life whilst the latter refers to the coherent expression of world-visions in great works of art and philosophy and even in the lives of exceptional individuals. These two planes complement each other, although potential consciousness may be easier to study since world-visions are expressed here with greater clarity and precision. Philosophical and artistic works are the individual and social expressions of world-visions, their content being determined by the maximum potential consciousness of the group and their form by the content for which the writer or thinker finds an adequate expression.[34]

The writer does not merely reflect the collective consciousness but, on the contrary, advances considerably the degree of structural coherence which the collective consciousness has itself achieved in a rough and ready fashion. The work of the artist, as an expression of this consciousness, may demonstrate to the group or class the directions its ideas and actions are taking, and thus bring out what the class is 'tending towards', the maximum possible awareness of the class. In the great work of art, the world-vision of the class reaches its fullest expression. The relationship between the class's practice and artistic production is reciprocal in the sense that the novel can help us to understand the class as well as being explicable in terms of the class's experiences.

Goldmann's method of understanding literary production, which he describes as 'genetic structuralism', treats the text both as the starting-point and the centre of research.[35] He begins by identifying certain structures within particular texts and then relates them to specific historical and social conditions, and to the world-visions of groups or classes associated with the writer. The emphasis then is on the text as a whole and history as a process. He does not dissolve the text into its milieu nor does he see it as a simple function of class-consciousness. Rejecting the orthodox Marxist view associated with Plekhanov,[36] which sees literature as a straightforward reflection of class interests and proffers an external explanation which refers to the aims of the class propagating the message contained in the text, Goldmann instead stresses the internal unity of the text as an expression of a world-vision. The great writer does not merely reflect the purposes of the group with which he is associated but actually identifies their aims and objectives. In developing Marx's notion of the limits of consciousness, Goldmann is able to ground ideas firmly in their social settings thereby avoiding a psychologistic conception of the acquisition of knowledge. At the same time he does not reduce ideas to material life since he is committed to a humanistic rather than a deterministic form of Marxism. His development of Marx's ideas in the notion of a world-vision serves as a possible bridge between Marx and Wittgenstein, via the Wittgensteinian idea of a world-picture.

Wittgenstein: world-pictures

The notion of a world-picture is developed in Wittgenstein's posthumously published work *On Certainty*, where he is concerned with Moore's refutation of philosophical scepticism.[37] Whilst Moore sought an indubitable standard of certainty in particular foundational truisms Wittgenstein emphasised that doubts can be raised only against a background of certainty and that this background does not rest on any external standard of indubitability. On the contrary it constitutes a world-picture which he describes as the 'inherited background against which I distinguish between true and false'.[38] It is also the background against which any particular belief may be understood in the sense that our beliefs form a system: 'When we first begin to *believe* anything, what we believe is not a single proposition, it is a whole system of propositions. (Light dawns gradually over the whole.)'[39] In so far as both Marx and Wittgenstein stress the totality and the internal structural relationships within the totality, we can discern a fundamental similarity between the Marxian notion of a world-view or world-vision and the Wittgensteinian notion of a *Weltbild*. One might argue that the Marxian world-view is Wittgenstein's world-vision given an historical content. Wittgenstein is concerned with the structural features of a world-picture which he sees as the background against which doubts can be raised. In drawing attention to the notion of a world-picture and its essential features, Wittgenstein is able to throw light on the processes involved in understanding and misunderstanding social relationships. Although in this sense Wittgenstein's world-picture does have sociological relevance, it was initially introduced in the course of an epistemological debate in which he tries to show that the logic of certainty and necessity are internal to specific activities rather than being derived from a foundational source of certitude as both Moore and his sceptical adversary believed. A world-picture is itself neither true nor false, but disputes concerning truth and falsity are possible only within its limited boundaries: 'But I did not get my picture of the world by satisfying myself of its correctness; nor do I have it because I am satisfied of its correctness'.[40] While questions may be raised within a world-picture, they cannot be raised about a world-picture. This was Moore's mistake: he saw no difference between such questions. Hence when dealing with the sceptic, he conceded that questions such as 'Does the external world exist?' were meaningful, whereas for Wittgenstein they were nonsensical, precisely because they doubted the framework within which meaningful doubts and questions could arise and be settled. Questions concerning the existence and pre-existence of unicorns are meaningful because they presuppose a world in which one could conduct an enquiry, but questions concerning the reality of the external world throw doubt on the meaning of enquiry itself and for that reason lie outside the scope of meaningful enquiry.

Wittgenstein's treatment of the 'problem of the external world' is very similar to the position taken by Marx in his 'Theses on Feuerbach' although Marx poses the question somewhat differently:

> The question whether objective truth can be attributed to human thinking is not a question of theory but is a *practical question*. Man must prove the truth, i.e. the reality and power, the this-sidedness of his thinking in practice. The dispute over the reality or non-reality of thinking that is isolated from practice is a purely *scholastic* question.[41]

He is very critical of those who merely 'interpret' the world without making any effort to transform it. For Marx, as for Wittgenstein, questions concerning the reality of the external world are meaningless and reflect the philosopher's voluntary isolation from ordinary life. Rather, the existence of the external world must be taken as given. In commenting on Marx's theses, Bukharin brings out well the absurdity of this particular philosophical chestnut:

> Practically – and, consequently, epistemologically – the external world is 'given' as the object of active influence on the part of social, historically developing man. The external world has its history. The relations growing up between subject and object are historical. The forms of these relations are historical. Practice itself and theory, the forms of active influence, and the forms of cognition, the 'modes of production' and 'the modes of conception', are historical. The question of the *existence* of the external world is categorically superfluous, since the reply is already evident, since the external world is 'given', just as practice itself is 'given'. Just for this reason in practical life there are no seekers after solipsism, there are no agnostics, no subjective idealists. Consequently epistemology, *including* praxiology, epistemology which *is* praxiology, must have its point of departure in the reality of the external world: not as a fiction, not as an illusion, not as a *hypothesis*, but as a basic fact.[42]

Not all propositions are as safe from doubt and the need for verification as those concerning the reality of the external world. Wittgenstein in *On Certainty* is anxious to dispel the rigidly cast distinction between logical necessity and empirical contingency. In doing so, he argues that the nature of human doubt and certainty is such that certain propositions which constitute the framework of a world-view must be exempt from enquiry, even though, from another standpoint, these propositions can be doubted:

> But what men consider reasonable or unreasonable alters. At certain periods men find reasonable what at other periods they found unreasonable. And vice versa.
>
> But is there no objective character here?
>
> *Very* intelligent and well-educated people believe in the story of creation in the Bible, while others hold it as proven false, and the grounds of the latter are well known to the former.[43]

> One cannot make experiments if there are not some things that one does not doubt. But that does not mean that one takes certain presuppositions on trust. When I write a letter and post it, I take it for granted that it will arrive – I expect this.[44]

Another example is the proposition that the earth is round. Long ago it was held to be flat. The various shades of opinion regarding the shape of the earth could be seen as incommensurable. A consideration of this question will reveal the absurdity of looking for an objective tribunal to which one can appeal. If the flat earth hypothesis were to have a grain of validity, practices such as cartography, satellite communication, space travel and so on would have to be abandoned. The roundness of the earth is too big a belief to nominate for investigation, since so many practices depend on it. In so far as the roundness of the earth is an assumption built into our calculations, it is a condition of enquiry not a subject of enquiry. Indeed, when discussing air traffic routes, for example, the question of whether the earth is flat is never raised, since within the context of the enquiry such a belief would be meaningless. As Wittgenstein says:

> We know that the earth is round. We have definitely ascertained that it is round.
>
> We shall stick to this opinion, unless our whole way of seeing nature changes. 'How do you know that?', – I believe it.[45]

In order to acquire an understanding of any phenomenon we need to grasp its relationships and connections with other phenomena:

> A main source of our failure to understand is that we do not *command a clear view* of the use of our words. – Our grammar is lacking in this sort of perspicuity. A perspicuous representation produces just that understanding which consists in 'seeing connexions'. Hence the importance of finding and inventing *intermediate cases.*
>
> The concept of a perspicuous representation is of fundamental significance for us. It earmarks the form of account we give, the way we look at things. (Is this a 'Weltanschauung?)[46]

That the boundaries of our world-pictures are subject to change as the forces of production change can be seen by reference to Wittgenstein's treatment of the proposition 'I have never been on the moon'. For Wittgenstein in 1950 questions concerning the truth of this proposition were alien to the world-picture of his time:

> What we believe depends on what we learn. We all believe that it isn't possible to get to the moon; but there might be people who believe that that is possible and that it sometimes happens. We say: these people do not know a lot that we know. And, let them be never so sure of their belief – they are wrong and we know it.
>
> If we compare our system of knowledge with theirs then theirs is evidently the poorer one by far.[47]

Of course, few people today, in the wake of the Apollo moonshots, would share his view, yet in 1950 he was correct. Given the level of technology and scientific knowledge of his time, he was right to say: '... Everything that I have seen or heard gives me the conviction that no man has ever been far from the earth. Nothing in my picture of the world speaks in favour of the opposite'.[48] Whilst the boundaries of a world-view have the necessary features of analytic propositions, they exhibit, nevertheless, certain qualities of contingency. Wittgenstein gives some indication of this in his analogy of the river bed:

> It might be imagined that some propositions, of the form of empirical propositions, were hardened and functioned as channels for such empirical propositions as were not hardened but fluid; and that this relation altered with time, in that fluid propositions hardened, and hard ones became fluid.[49]
>
> The mythology may change back into a state of flux, the river-bed of thoughts may shift. But I distinguish between the movement of the waters on the river-bed and the shift of the bed itself; though there is not a sharp division of the one from the other.[50]
>
> But if someone were to say 'So logic too is an empirical science' he would be wrong. Yet this is right: the same proposition may get treated at one time as something to test by experience, at another as a rule of testing.[51]
>
> And the bank of that river consists partly of hard rock, subject to no alteration or only to an imperceptible one, partly of sand, which now in one place now in another gets washed away, or deposited.[52]

Wittgenstein's model here is that of a 'guiding framework' whose boundaries can shift. In saying that even the bed of the river may move, Wittgenstein is clearly rejecting what may be called a foundationalist approach in which a number of basic assumptions are identified as forming the foundations of our knowledge.[53]

For Wittgenstein, a world-picture is the common ground that must be shared with others for communication to be possible. In this sense it constitutes the limits of the world for the group who share that world-picture. But these limits or boundaries are by no means fixed and may fluctuate considerably. This aspect of world-pictures may be illustrated by the notion of *Vorwissen* (pre-knowledge) employed by Von Wright.[54] He points out that each language-game or activity is a fragment of the player's *Vorwissen*, by which he means the system of propositions which are taken for granted as a condition for judgements, investigations and experiments. In so far as they stand fast within any given situation, we cannot apply the term 'knowledge' to them. The certainty of such forms of *Vorwissen* as, for example, 'the world has existed for many years', is not proven by empirical investigation into the past but rather is a presupposition of *any* historical knowledge. As Wittgenstein remarks: 'Perhaps what is inexpressible (what I find mysterious and am not able to express) is the background against which whatever I could express has its meaning'.[55] In numerous examples he demonstrates how the various forms of *Vorwissen* are acquired thereby revealing the limits to scientific inquiry and showing how both Moore and his sceptical adversaries had transgressed them. Consider Wittgenstein's treatment of questions raised by Moore concerning the reality of his hand:

> We teach a child 'that is your hand', not 'that is perhaps (or "probably") your hand'. That is how a child learns the innumerable language-games that are concerned with his hand. An investigation or question 'whether this is really a hand' never occurs to him. Nor, on the other hand, does he learn that he *knows* that this is a hand.
>
> Only in certain cases is it possible to make an investigation 'is that really a hand?' (or 'my hand'). For 'I doubt whether that is really my (or a) hand' makes no sense without some more precise determination. One cannot tell from these words alone whether any doubt at all is meant – nor what kind of doubt.[56]

In making this point Wittgenstein emphasises the way in which children learn: 'Children do not learn that books exist, that armchairs exist, etc. etc. – they learn to fetch books, sit in armchairs, etc. etc.'[57] For Wittgenstein the limits to enquiry, the forms of *Vorwissen*, are a built-in condition of there being any enquiry. As such they are beyond the scope of investigation. The forms of *Vorwissen* are relative to human activity. Whilst there are certain propositions beyond doubt or proof in any forms of human activity, such as propositions concerning the reality of the external world, there are others which are affected by changes in social life. It is in this area that the logical boundaries governing what can be said are set by social practices. At the basis of our world-picture, says Wittgenstein, is a way of acting: 'It is not a kind of *seeing* on our part; it is our *acting* which lies at the bottom of the language-game'.[58] Many of our doubts and certainties are grounded in a particular way of life. As Wittgenstein says, 'My *life* consists in my being content to accept many things'.[59] Our certainty expresses itself in the way we act.

If a world-picture refers to the agreements in judgements and reactions necessary for communication to be possible, what will happen when different world-pictures clash? Without this common background there will be no overt disagreement but mutual incomprehension. If mutual understanding is possible only among those who share the same world-view, then how is it possible for adherents of one world-view to communicate to another and to convince them that their own world-view is a better one? Wittgenstein considers this question in relation to the problem of understanding a society whose members consult oracles instead of scientists:

> Is it wrong for me to be guided in my actions by the propositions of physics? Am I to say I have no good ground for doing so? Isn't precisely this what we call a 'good ground'?[60]

> Supposing we met people who did not regard that as a telling reason. Now, how do we imagine this? Instead of the physicist, they consult an oracle. (And for that we

consider them primitive.) Is it wrong for them to consult an oracle and be guided by it? – If we call this 'wrong' aren't we using our language-game as a base from which to *combat* theirs?[61]

And are we right or wrong to combat it? Of course there are all sorts of slogans which will be used to support our proceedings.[62]

Where two principles really do meet which cannot be reconciled with one another, then each man declares the other a fool and a heretic.[63]

I said I would 'combat' the other man, – but wouldn't I give him *reasons*? Certainly: but how far do they go? At the end of reasons comes *persuasion*. (Think what happens when missionaries convert natives.)[64]

Implicit in Wittgenstein's remarks is the idea that different world-pictures may not judge each other since they lack an external tribunal, but this is not to deny that language-games may change.[65] As he says:

But how many kinds of sentence are there? Say assertion, question and command? – There are *countless* kinds; countless different kinds of use of what we call 'symbols', 'words', 'sentences'. And this multiplicity is not something fixed, given once for all; but new types of language, new language-games, as we may say, come into existence, and others become obsolete and get forgotten. (We can get a *rough picture* of this from the changes in mathematics.)

Here the term 'language-*game*' is meant to bring into prominence the fact that the *speaking* of language is part of an activity, or of a form of life ....[66]

But if language-games are not permitted to judge each other, where is the judgement to come from to lead to change? Not, says Wittgenstein, from philosophy:

Philosophy may in no way interfere with the actual use of language; it can in the end only describe it.

For it cannot give it any foundation either.

It leaves everything as it is.[67]

But this raises problems, as Bartley says: 'if conflicting language-games or forms of life are not themselves permitted to initiate grammatical change by sitting in judgment one on the other, then how *does* such change get started? And how is it to be evaluated?'.[68]

Although Wittgenstein fails to answer this question explicitly, his remarks concerning the nature of grammar, to be discussed in the next chapter, throw some light on the question of the limits to social change. He certainly does not rule out the possibility of criticism of world-views and thereby the form of life in which the world-view is grounded. In his disparaging comments on the idea of a man visiting the moon, he is attacking the world-view in which this statement would make sense, and in doing so he echoes Lukács's point that the historical standpoint imposes limits on world-views.[69] But whilst Wittgenstein acknowledges that criticism is possible and that language-games may change, he is hostile to the participation of philosophy in such change. His hostility is anticipated by Hegel in his Preface to the *Philosophy of Right*: 'When philosophy paints its grey in grey, then has a shape of life grown old. By philosophy's grey in grey it cannot be rejuvenated but only understood. The owl of Minerva spreads its wings only with the falling of the dusk'.[70] Like Hegel, Wittgenstein implies that philosophy – which reflects the real – cannot provide the blueprints for a reality which has not yet come into being. At a superficial level these remarks could indicate a form of conservatism in Wittgenstein, just as Hegel's remarks have been taken as a justification of the Prussian state. Yet Wittgenstein is simply questioning the instrumental separation of theory (philosophy) and practice. His remarks reveal the hollowness of a contemplative philosophy attacked by Marx in his famous 'Eleventh thesis on Feuerbach': 'The philosophers have only *interpreted* the world, in various ways, the point is to *change* it'.[71] This brings to mind the apocryphal story of Wittgenstein responding to this thesis by saying 'Let them try', which suggests that Wittgenstein was not advocating interpreting at the expense of changing the world but expressing doubt regarding the possibility of understanding and hence showing his disparagement of philosophy divorced from the real world. In urging his disciples to return to ordinary usage, Wittgenstein is arguably making a similar point to Engels who in 'Ludwig Feuerbach and the end of classical German philosophy', points out that only the working class remains capable of developing a theoretical understanding of the world since it is not concerned with profit or advancement. In fact, as objective science develops it moves closer to the interests of the working class. As he says, 'The German working-class movement is the inheritor of German classical philosophy'.[72]

From the above discussion we can discern a number of similarities between the Marxian notion of a world-view or world-vision and Wittgenstein's notion of a world-picture, which serve to distance Marx and Wittgenstein from the picture of ideology presupposed by the essence–appearance distinction. For Marx and Wittgenstein we understand phenomena by examining their interrelationships within a totality.[73] Rather than trying to understand beliefs, ideas or judgements in isolation, they see them as part of a network or system of beliefs or ideas which add up to a world-picture or world-view. Thus, according to Cornforth, the Marxian dialectic is to be understood in terms of this emphasis on interrelationships:

> It is generally agreed among Marxists that dialectics has to do with understanding things in their inter-relations and changes, as opposed to the 'metaphysical' way of considering things separately, out of relationship and in abstraction from their

> changes. Evidently, to get a concrete picture of any phenomenon we must assemble the available information in a way that adequately reflects the actual interconnections and motion of things, and thus understand the separate properties of things, and their temporary states, as products of processes of interaction and change. The dialectical approach consists in doing this – its 'laws' are the laws for doing it. As Lenin observed, the essence of dialectics is 'the concrete analysis of concrete conditions'.[74]

For Marx the mode of production was the framework within which all other features of social life could be explained and is therefore analogous to Wittgenstein's notion of a form of life. Each mode of production or 'form of life' generates ideas which articulate the experience of groups or classes. These ideas constitute the world-view which can only be understood in relation to the form of life within which it emerges. Hence, both stress the need to study the interrelationships or connections between phenomena. Wittgenstein's main concern, of course, was with the epistemological questions arising from these interrelationships, but since his death attempts have been made to apply his ideas to such diverse and subject-areas such as morality, art, religion and justice. But unlike the work of Marx and his followers, this has not yet extended to a social critique.

In postulating a close relationship between ideas and form of life, Marx and Wittgenstein assign a considerable degree of autonomy to ideas. This autonomy is reflected in Goldmann's distinction between real and potential consciousness. Facing the problem of giving a sociological account of literary creativity, he argues that the writer *advances* the consciousness of his class rather than simply *reflecting* it. Yet at the same time both Marx and Wittgenstein accept that one's membership of a group or class imposes limits on one's consciousness. Goldmann illustrates this point by reference to seventeenth- and eighteenth-century French literature whilst Wittgenstein is concerned with epistemological questions. But in neither case is the notion of limits to be understood in a crude coercive sense. Rather it draws attention to the internal relationship between ideas and social life. Nor are the limits static. The limits may change over time as the way of life changes. Hence we saw earlier how Marx points out that the standards of justice vary according to each mode of production. A world-view or world-picture is not a closed system of thought but rather the framework within which innovations have meaning. Indeed the idea of progress from one way of life to another constitutes an important facet of Wittgenstein's thought.

Whilst the Hegelian notion of world-view represents an advance on the essence–appearance account of ideology in so far as it rejects the use of the abstract individual in formulating a theory of knowledge, it none the less raises a number of problems. Firstly, if we accept that the form of life imposes limits on consciousness, what are the possibilities for social change? Secondly, if we accept that each world-view is a coherent entity with its own standards of rationality, morality and intelligiblity, what are we to make of disputes between competing world-views? How are we to decide which one is superior? If we align knowledge and reality with class interests, are we ruling out the possibility of an objective account of reality? These problems will be explored in the following chapters.

Notes to Chapter IV

[1] L. Goldmann, *The Hidden God* (London: Routledge and Kegan Paul, 1964); 'The sociology of literature', *International Social Science Journal* XI, 4.

[2] L. Wittgenstein, *On Certainty* (Oxford: Basil Blackwell, 1969).

[3] J. Mepham, 'The theory of ideology in *Capital*'.

[4] K. Marx, *Grundrisse* (London: Pelican, 1973) p. 265.

[5] K. Marx, *Capital* III, p. 809.

[6] K. Marx, *Grundrisse*, p. 84.

[7] *Ibid.*, p. 83.

[8] *Ibid.*, p. 83.

[9] *Ibid.*, p. 84.

[10] *Ibid.*, p. 87.

[11] *Ibid.*, p. 85.

[12] N. I. Bukharin, 'Theory and practice from the standpoint of dialectical materialism', *Science at the Crossroads*, p. 18.

[13] *Ibid.*, p. 22.

[14] P. Winch, 'Popper and scientific method in the social sciences', *The Philosophy of Karl Popper*, ed. P. A. Schilpp (la Salle, Ill.: Open Court, 1974) pp. 889–904.

[15] L. Wittgenstein, *op. cit.*, 402. (References to works by Wittgenstein are to paragraphs unless otherwise indicated.)

[16] L. Wittgenstein, *Philosophical Investigations*, 528.

[17] *Ibid.*, 529.

[18] K. Marx, *Grundrisse; The Poverty of Philosophy* (Moscow: Foreign Languages Publishing House, 1956).

[19] L. Goldmann, *Power and Humanism* (Nottingham: Spokesman, 1974), pp. 40–7.

[20] *Ibid.*, p. 47.

[21] K. Marx, 'Economic and philosophic manuscripts of 1844', *Collected Works* III, p. 299.

[22] C. Gould, *Marx's Social Ontology* (Cambridge, Mass.: MIT Press, 1978), p. 35.

[23] *Ibid.*, p. 38.

[24] G. Lukács, 'The Marxism of Rosa Luxemburg', *History and Class Consciousness*, p. 28.

[25] G. Lukács, 'What is orthodox Marxism?', *History and Class Consciousness*, pp. 1–26.

[26] L. Goldmann, *The Hidden God*, p. 17.

[27] L. Goldmann, *The Human Sciences and Philosophy* (London: Jonathan Cape, 1969).

[28] J.-J. Rousseau, *The Social Contract* (London: Penguin, 1968).

[29] K. Marx, *The Eighteenth Brumaire of Louis Bonaparte* (Moscow: Progress Publishers, 1967), pp. 40–1.

[30] This point is also made by C. Taylor in 'Interpretation and the sciences of man', *Man and World* (1973) pp. 1–31.

[31] L. Goldmann, *Power and Humanism*, p. 3.

[32] *Ibid.*, pp. 3–4.

[33] L. Goldmann, *The Human Sciences and Philosophy*.

[34] *Ibid.*

[35] The centrality of the text has also been emphasised by philosophers influenced by the later Wittgenstein. See, for example, R. Beardsmore *Art and Morality* (London: Macmillan, 1971).

[36] G. Plekhanov, *Art and Social Life* (1912) (London: Lawrence and Wishart, 1953).

[37] L. Wittgenstein, *On Certainty*; this work constituted a reply to the following papers of G. E. Moore, 'A defence of commonsense' and 'A proof of an external world'. available in *Philosophical Papers* (London: Allen and Unwin, 1959). The significance of Wittgenstein's work in *On Certainty* can be seen in relation to the search for the kind of certainty from which the essence–appearance dichotomy derives its force. In order to commit oneself to the search for an underlying structure of reality, the traditional ploy consists of casting doubt on the reality of the world around us. We are then asked to consider the nature of a hidden realm of certainty beneath the phenomenal forms. Moore's 'refutation' of scepticism consisted of the assembling of what he thought was empirical evidence. Sceptical arguments that we can never know the reality of external objects were countered by Moore by the exhibition of one of his hands. But this placed Moore in the same metaphysical standpoint as the sceptic, asserting facts that the others were denying. Wittgenstein's originality lies in his demonstration that the truisms employed by Moore to refute scepticism – and with it the search for an indubitable realm of truth – belong to the sphere of *Vorwissen*. Scepticism could be routed not by the postulation of a foundational realm of empirical or logical certainty but by an appeal to ordinary practice.

[38] L. Wittgenstein, *op. cit.*, 94.

[39] *Ibid.*, 141.

[40] *Ibid.*, 94.

[41] K. Marx, 'Second Thesis on Feuerbach'.

[42] N. Bukharin, 'Theory and practice from the standpoint of dialectical materialism', p. 16.

[43] L. Wittgenstein, *op. cit.*, 336.

[44] *Ibid.*, 337.

[45] *Ibid.*, 291.

[46] L. Wittgenstein, *Philosophical Investigations*, I, 122.

[47] L. Wittgenstein, *On Certainty*, 286.

[48] *Ibid.*, 93.

[49] *Ibid.*, 96.

[50] *Ibid.*, 97.

[51] *Ibid.*, 98.

[52] *Ibid.*, 99.

[53] An interesting variation of this view is advanced by Popper in *The Logic of Scientific Discovery* (London: Hutchinson, 1959), although the foundations in Popper's case are basic statements whereas Wittgenstein emphasises instead the relationships between the various aspects of a world-picture.

[54] G. H. von Wright, 'Wittgenstein's *On Certainty*', *Problems in the Theory of Knowledge* (The Hague: Martinus Nijhoff, 1970).

[55] L. Wittgenstein, *Culture and Value* (Oxford: Basil Blackwell, 1980), p. 16e.

[56] L. Wittgenstein, *On Certainty*, 374, 372.

[57] *Ibid.*, 476.

[58] *Ibid.*, 204.

[59] *Ibid.*, 344.

[60] *Ibid.*, 608.

[61] *Ibid.*, 609.

[62] *Ibid.*, 610.

[63] *Ibid.*, 611.

[64] *Ibid.*, 612.

[65] Wittgenstein likens the move from one language-game or world-picture to another to a *Gestalt* switch. See *Philosophical Investigations*, II, xi, p. 208.

[66] L. Wittgenstein, *ibid.*, 23.

[67] *Ibid.*, 124

[68] W. W. Bartley III, *Wittgenstein* (London: Quartet Books, 1974), p. 124.

[69] G. Lukács, 'Reification and the consciousness of the proletariat', *History and Class Consciousness*.

[70] G. W. F. Hegel, Preface to *Philosophy of Right*, p. 3.

[71] K. Marx, 'Eleventh Thesis on Feuerbach'.

[72] F. Engels, 'Ludwig Feuerbach and the end of classical German philosophy', *Marx and Engels: Basic Writings*, p. 282.

[73] See L. Wittgenstein, *Philosophical Investigations*, I, 122. Wittgenstein's work could be seen as a demonstration of the principle of totality when he emphasises that the meaning of words is to be understood in terms of their use in a particular context. This view was not confined to his later work but played an important role in the *Tractatus* where he argues 'Only propositions have sense; only in the nexus of a proposition does a name have meaning' (3. 3). *Tractatus Logico-Philosophicus* (London: Routledge and Kegan Paul, 1961).

[74] M. Cornforth, *Marxism and the Linguistic Philosophy* (London: Lawrence and Wishart, 1965), p. 292.

V

Nature and convention

Given the limitations on consciousness we have identified what kinds of changes are possible within a particular form of life?[1] For Hegel, Marx and some contemporary Wittgensteinians, notably Winch, any novelty is constrained by existing traditions. Marx makes this point forcibly in the *Eighteenth Brumaire*:

> Men make their own history, but they do not make it just as they please; they do not make it under circumstances chosen by themselves, but under circumstances directly encountered, given and transmitted from the past. The tradition of all the dead generations weighs like a nightmare on the brain of the living.[2]

We shall therefore examine the question of the limits to social change in terms of the nature–convention distinction. Both Marx and Wittgenstein might be seen as conventionalists in the sense that both reject the view that certain phenomena – whether social institutions or scientific laws – are *in the nature of things* and cannot be changed. However, a number of different varieties of conventionalism may be distinguished:[3] in the philosophy of science, for example, conventionalism has arisen in response to the question 'what are the limits to acceptable theories?'. The conventionalist would argue that these limits are a matter of social convention rather than determined by the natural world. Parallel arguments may be found in the sphere of morality. Following a brief discussion of the problems raised by the nature–convention distinction in science and morality, we shall consider the epistemological and semantic implications of this distinction, drawing heavily from Wittgenstein's contribution to this question. It will be argued that the problem of conventionalism is to some extent a pseudo-problem and that instead of examining unlimited possibilities of new forms of social life, we need to look at the kinds of activities that actually exist *in* societies and see what opportunities for change are conceivable on the basis of those activities.

Conventionalism in science is usually associated with Poincaré who argued that scientific propositions are in fact artificial creations rather than descriptions of the world arrived at through experiment and investigation.[4] We accept them as true not because we are forced to do so through overwhelming evidence (the realist position) but because they are useful or convenient or even because they have aesthetic appeal. Another popular conventionalist view is that the truth of a scientific theory is analytical and therefore immune to refutation by experience.[5] This view was held by Le Roy who argued that individual cases may be classified as falling or not falling under the general law. But there is no question of discarding the law if one meets with empirical evidence which contradicts it. The law governing the free fall of bodies, for example, would be seen as an analytic proposition which merely defines free fall. If we see a body falling at a different rate of acceleration than anticipated by the law, we would not reject the law but simply say that what we see is not free fall. The standards for judging what should go under the law are man-made agreements adopted in the process of concept formation rather than strictly determined by the structure of the natural world.[6]

Support for conventionalism may also be found in the work of Popper who, although critical of conventionalism, emphasises in *The Logic of Scientific Discovery* that basic statements in science are accepted as a result of decision and agreement:

> From a logical point of view, the testing of a theory depends upon basic statements whose acceptance or rejection, in its turn, depends upon our *decisions*. Thus it is *decisions* which settle the fate of theories. To this extent my answer to the question 'how do we select a theory?' resembles that given by the conventionalist; and like him I say that this choice is in part determined by considerations of utility.[7]

These decisions are conventions in so far as they are reached in accordance with a rule-governed procedure. Popper is also committed to the primacy of theory over the 'facts' of experience.[8] But his version of conventionalism is limited by his insistence on a strict methodology which weeds out unacceptable theories. In arguing that theories must be capable of being falsified before they can count as scientific, he differs from conventionalists like Poincaré for whom theories could achieve scientific status simply by being defined as such.[9] Nevertheless, despite Popper's denial of a conventionalist position, many of his views point in that direction. His emphasis on decisions, for example, would seem to place him in the conventionalist camp. Furthermore, he claims that basic statements may be open to challenge at any time since they are based on conventions even though, for pragmatic reasons, we cannot challenge all the basic statements at any one time.[10]

Popper also offers a quasi-conventionalist view of morality in *The Open Society* where he argues that morality is subject to decisions.[11] As we noted earlier (Chapter III), problems arise with such a decisionist theory of morality. To begin with, moral changes do not occur as a direct result of decisions on the part of individuals. Of course, moral ideas may change and concepts may come to be applied in new ways, leading to changes in moral actions. But while these changes are linked with people's decisions they are not 'decided upon' as Popper suggests. For a moral decision can be made only within the context of a particular world-view or moral practice whereas a morality cannot be based on decisions. One might decide to become a good Catholic, trade-unionist or politician but the morality entailed by these institutions is not a matter of decision. In Wittgensteinian terms we make decisions within a particular grammar but we do not choose the grammar. Secondly, the conventionalist or decisionist account of morality tends to reduce the sphere of morality to the irrational. For Popper, morality lies outside rational enquiry since it emerges from decisions which emanate from the individual conscience. This emphasis on decisions rests on an acceptance of the fact–value distinction which, as we observed earlier, is rejected by both Marxists and Wittgensteinians.[12] Just as the Wittgensteinian notion of a moral practice may cast light on the question of moral change, so Wittgenstein's approach to the nature–convention question can further our understanding of the limits to social change. Although Wittgenstein's approach may bear a superficial resemblance to conventionalism, it will be argued that he transcends both conventionalism and its opposite, naturalism. He deals with this question in the context of an analysis of the relationship between language and reality.

Language and reality

The question of whether reality is determined by thought and language or whether it imposes its form upon thought and language was of central importance to Wittgenstein, although as his philosophical ideas developed, his solution to this problem changed.[13] Thus in the later work, he 'abandoned the idea that the structure of reality determines the structure of language, and suggested that it is really the other way round: our language determines our view of reality, because we see things through it'.[14] Wittgenstein has been described as a conventionalist because his account of the relationship between language and the world could be seen as an implicit attack on Platonic or Russellian realism, in so far as he challenges the assumption common to Russell, Frege and his own *Tractatus* that the meaning of a word is determined by the object to which it refers: 'For a *large* class of cases – though not for all – in which we employ the word 'meaning' it can be defined thus: the meaning of a word is its use in the language'.[15] In his later writings Wittgenstein held that the facts do not serve as the foundation of language any more than language serves as the foundation of our knowledge of reality. Both poles of this false antinomy assume that one either commences endowed with a knowledge of all the facts from which one then infers a language, or that one begins with a completed language from within which one determines the facts. Language for Wittgenstein, as for Marx, is an activity in which one engages when interacting with the natural world, imposing a structure on it. The world may be presented to us in an organised fashion but this classification and organisation is undertaken and acquired in learning the language, which is an activity inseparable from learning how to live in the world. The meaning of a word cannot be reduced to the object it signifies nor to the intention on the part of the speaker.[16] Rather, the meaning of a word is determined by the rules of usage. This is not to say that Wittgenstein replaces the traditional 'objects' of the realist with the formal rules of language and syntax. He is principally concerned with what we *do* with language rather than what language *is*. This emerges clearly in Wittgenstein's comparison of language with tools, developed in the *Philosophical Investigations*:

> Think of the tools in a tool-box; there is a hammer, pliers, a saw, a screw-driver, a rule, a glue-pot, glue, nails and screws. – The function of words are as diverse as the functions of these objects. (And in both cases there are similarities).[17]

> But a machine surely cannot think! – Is that an empirical statement? No. We only say of a human being and what is like one that it thinks. We also say it of dolls and no doubt of spirits too. Look at the word 'to think' as a tool.[18]

For Wittgenstein language is part of the practice of social life: 'Here the term "language-*game*" is meant to bring into prominence the fact that the *speaking* of language is part of an activity, or of a form of life'.[19] By emphasising the use of words, he moves away from passive theories of language and closer to Marxism. Language is not simply read off from reality, but is part of the reality-creating process. It does not express a community's *beliefs* about reality nor does it attempt to describe reality but people do so *in* the language that they speak. This point is developed by Winch who argues that 'Reality is not what gives language sense. What is real and what is unreal shows itself *in* the sense that language has'.[20] The relationship between language and reality does not refer to the relation between descriptions and the object of those descriptions, for 'the grammar of a language is not a theory about the nature of reality, even though new factual discoveries and theoretical developments may lead to grammatical changes'.[21] Winch here echoes Wittgenstein's remark in *Culture and Value* that 'The limit of language is shown by its being impossible to describe the fact which corresponds to (is the translation of) a sentence, without simply repeating the sentence ...'.[22]

While our view of nature does not determine what nature is, at the same time language and reality, or nature, are related in the sense that the real *shows itself* in the sense that language has. For this reason Winch distinguishes between 'the beliefs people hold and the language in which those beliefs are expressed and which makes them possible'.[23] He therefore rejects the idea that the grammar of a language constitutes the expression of beliefs or theories about the world which are open to verification or falsification through an examination of what the world is like. But this distinction between the beliefs people hold and the language in which they express these beliefs is not always clear-cut:

> The grammar of the word 'pain' finds expression in what we say about the pains ... of particular people ... But what we mean by 'pain' is not the sum of our particular beliefs about the ... pains ... of particular people ....[24]

> What the Azande mean by their word for 'oracle' is not the sum of their particular beliefs about oracles.[25]

He concludes that if, at some future point in time, the Azande discard their belief in oracles this need not be because those beliefs have been refuted by evidence that the world contains no witches, any more than the secularisation of modern society is a consequence of the proof that God does not exist. The reality of Zande oracles, like Western religious practices, is not determined by the facts but by the *grammar* in which these facts are expressed. The problem for the anthropologist studying an alien society is to distinguish the realm of grammar from the realm of belief. The notion of grammar is also useful for the Marxist in giving an account of social change.

Grammar and grammatical propositions

An understanding of the notion of grammar may be gleaned from remarks on this subject scattered throughout Wittgenstein's texts. For Wittgenstein, reality cannot be construed as standing outside our conceptual framework: it is only within the conceptions that make up our world-picture that we can talk of certain things being real or unreal, for 'Like everything else metaphysical the harmony between thought and reality is to be found in the grammar of the language'.[26] He arrives at his notion of grammar through an examination of the limits of language. Certain expressions, he says, may be acceptable syntactically yet still meaningless within our language and way of life. An example would be the question 'where does the fire go when it goes out?', which calls attention to the grammatical limits for the concept 'fire'. Similarly the grammar of colour language-games is bounded by grammatical positions such as 'White is lighter than black' or 'Green and blue cannot be in the same place simultaneously'.[27] Whilst in themselves these propositions are trivial and uninformative, they reflect certain conventions for the employment of their component terms. From within a particular world-view, these grammatical propositions may appear as necessarily true in the sense that we cannot imagine them to be otherwise. Superficially they are akin to analytical propositions, largely due to the force with which they are held. But even though grammatical propositions may have a cast-iron rigidity within their respective language-games, they can change. Moreover, given that they have the peculiar property of appearing both certain and open to factual consideration, they have been likened to synthetic *a priori* propositions. But this has been rightly denied by Brown who, referring to a previous discussion of grammatical propositions, comments:

> It may seem, therefore, that I am undertaking to defend *synthetic a priori* truth. But this is not so. For in the first place I do not wish to accept the rigid structure of relations between concepts which is implied by that sense of 'analytic' normally contrasted with ... 'synthetic'. In the second place I have not wished to say that grammatical claims could be *known* to be true, still less that they could be known to be true quite apart from any experience. Both the terms 'synthetic' and the terms 'a priori' are therefore out of place.[28]

Because the grammatical remarks constitute the boundaries of our world-picture they are neither true nor false but provide the background against which we can raise questions of truth or falsity. Their capacity for change reflects the possibility of a different world-view, not merely a set of contrary facts.

A tendency prevails in much modern philosophy, however, to confuse the rules of a given activity with the grammar of an activity. Searle, for example, has been accused by Schwyzer of assuming that rules define a particular activity.[29] Against this, Schwyzer argues that whilst activities may be governed by rules as, for example, in the case of chess, the rules governing the moves do not define the meaning of the game in any particular culture. What it makes sense to say about chess, its significance in a specific form of life, is what Wittgenstein means by 'grammar' and this cannot be reduced to the rules: whilst rules do not socially define an activity, the grammar does. Searle's emphasis on constitutive rules, as rules defining an activity, therefore tends to obscure the distinction between rules and grammar. This is illustrated by Schwyzer, with reference to the hypothetical example of Ruritania where, he says, chess is played once a year by priests in order to determine the will of the gods. While in this culture the playing of chess is a sacred rite, this information is not contained in the rules of the game. As outsiders we may understand the moves players make without understanding the meaning or significance of the game in that culture; for the grammar of chess, what it makes sense to say about chess and the reactions of people to it, is concerned not with what happens on the board but with the role that chess has in that form of life.

The rules cannot be conflated with the grammar since the grammar refers to the meaning of an activity and not simply the rules for conducting the activity. As Schwyzer says: 'Playing chess does not *consist* in acting in accordance with the rules',[30] for the rules cannot establish what it means to play chess. The meaning of chess is embodied in the grammar of an activity but the grammar cannot be reduced to the rules nor is an account of grammar exhausted by reference to the rules. This is true not merely of hypothetical cases like chess in Ruritania but also in most cases where we talk of rule-governed practices or institutions. The rules of a practice do not tell us what the practice is or what it *means* to those governed by the rules. An activity needs to be set in a wider context in order for its grammar to be appreciated.

Whilst Schwyzer's distinction between rules and grammar may be of value in understanding social change, one should not conclude that the rules and grammar of an activity must always be rigidly separated. Often the rules and grammar are more closely connected than Schwyzer's account would suggest. The film *Rollerball* may serve to illustrate this point. The game of rollerball had the explicit social purpose of demonstrating that individual effort was futile in a corporate society. The rules of the game prescribed that one could score points by catching a rapidly-moving ball and placing it into a chute before the opposing side. Although dangerous, the game was regulated by penalty clauses and a time limit to prevent too much bloodshed. However, with the emergence of superstars the corporate ethos was threatened. To remedy this challenge plans were formulated to change the rules so that the probable fatality of the superstars would be increased. These changes amounted to the removal of penalty and substitution clauses from what was already a physically demanding game. Finally, when the time limit was removed an observer remarked that it was no longer a game. In this case the rules were changed so dramatically that the grammar of the game itself was affected. Before the change it was possible to distinguish the rules from the grammar. Following the introduction of the new rules, one could no longer speak of it as a game. It had become an attempt to assassinate a potential leader of discontent. In this example, the distinction between rules and grammar is not as clear-cut as Schwyzer suggests, since changes in the rules initiated changes in the grammar of the activity from a game to a defence of a corporate state against a specific attack. However, it should be noted that an understanding of both the rules and the grammatical change in this case is only explicable in terms of the political role of the game in the society portrayed.

Conceptual or grammatical change

It has been argued that the certainty of grammatical propositions is guaranteed because they constitute the framework of meaning in a language game. In so far as human activities or 'modes of production' can change, so too can the conventions signified by grammatical propositions change. Wittgenstein ties conceptual or grammatical change closely to social change, to changes in human activities. An examination of grammatical change can therefore help to throw light on the question of the limits to social change. An interesting example of conceptual or grammatical change is the idea of a 'law of nature' cited by both Toulmin and Brown, both of whom closely follow Wittgenstein in formulating this idea.[31] Toulmin points out that this expression has ceased to be associated with theology in the sense of referring to the will of a Creator. Indeed, we can now accept the idea of a 'law of nature' as a 'working' assumption. Similarly, Brown remarks that:

> We no longer assume, in describing something as a 'law of nature' or a 'natural law', that it has been ordained by some higher being. And this seems to be a case where a change in our use of an expression reflects a conceptual change. For at one time people did believe that order in the course of events was to be attributed to the governing hand of a providence. Indeed, it is difficult to see how the word 'law' could have been applied to the course of events at all, had this not been so ... Part of what is involved here is the recognition that theological considerations are not relevant to the conduct of scientific inquiry.[32]

A crude conventionalist account of this change might see it as simply a change in linguistic terminology. In this case the truth of the proposition expressed by the word 'natural law' would remain unaffected. But when we are dealing with the move from a belief in divine providence to a confidence in scientific laws we are referring to something more than a mere change in terminology. What we are dealing with here is the far greater phenomenon of the secularisation of the Western world which accompanied the emergence of a new world-view which deemed that religious concepts were no longer appropriate rather than incorrect or falsified.[33] We can see from this example that conceptual or grammatical changes concern changes in people's outlook and in the lives they lead. Nor is a conceptual change accounted for simply in terms of the recognition of new facts. What is involved is what Brown calls insight, that is, seeing matters in a new light. But whilst the grammar may change within each world-view, in each case the grammatical propositions which mark the conceptual boundaries are accepted as certain. As Brown says: '"grammatical" claims may be thought of as in a sense "necessarily" true. To accept a claim as true in this way is to accept it as one which could not *conceivably* be false'.[34] It is this same sense of necessary truth and conceivability that is involved in Marx's claim that the intellectual representatives of a class do not get beyond the limits in thought that the class gets beyond in practice.

From within its world-view, certain boundaries are drawn concerning what it makes sense to say and do. Yet the conventionality of grammar can be seen when we recall that for the early nineteenth-century mind, conflict between bourgeois and proletarian was inconceivable, but decades later it was not only conceivable but the subject of spirited discussion.[35] An understanding of the limits of class-consciousness in terms of world-views lends itself to an explanation in terms of Wittgenstein's notion of grammar. We could describe the two views of class conflict as expressing different grammars. Moreover, the apparently analytical nature of grammatical propositions can explain the nature of incommensurability involved in a clash of world-views. The mutual incomprehension characteristic of confrontations between Marxist and non-Marxist world-views reveals conflicting systems of grammatical propositions with distinct rules which cannot be compared. That this can happen *within* a particular culture as well as between diverse cultures reflects the arbitrariness of a grammar of meaning.

The introduction of a new grammar

An essential feature of Marxist practice is the attempt to transform the world which is bound up with the adoption of a new world-view with its own grammar. An examination of the limits of grammatical change may therefore throw light on the possibility of achieving a Marxist transformation of society and the extent to which a Marxist world-view and way of life is fashioned by the grammar of the world-view preceeding it. With the passing of time several 'Marxist' revolutions have not exhibited such a dramatic break with the past as their participants anticipated. This seems to suggest that world-views are never so far apart that their grammatical rules are incompatible or absolutely exclusive despite their apparent incommensurability. It also indicates that the grammar of one world-view limits, to a certain extent, the range of options open to another world-view even though, at the time of change, it has the appearance of a total rupture. An examination of the grammar of a society therefore entails a discussion of the possibilities for grammatical and therefore social change. The way in which Winch implicitly draws the limits of grammatical alternatives when he considers the possibility of understanding a different system of grammar will be referred to in this context.

Implicit in Winch's work is the view that the grammatical differences between Zande witchcraft practices and modern Western culture are such that the adoption of the former by Western culture is unintelligible.[36] Even if one could practice Zande witchcraft according to the rule-book, one would not be entering into the grammar of that practice. 'Culture', says Winch, 'sets limits to what an individual can intelligibly be said to be doing' and in the absence of Zande culture from which the grammar of witchcraft is derived, the adoption of such practices would be little more than a charade.[37] Conversely, there is nothing in Western practices upon which one could base a criticism of Zande witchcraft. This view, and the epistemological model on which it rests, can be criticised, as we shall see later, for its implicit conservatism and resistance to social change. Nevertheless, in a reply to his critics, Winch argues that whilst change is not ruled out on his model, it must be limited by one's present world-view: 'This is not to say that there cannot be new cultural developments ... but what can count as a new development is also limited by the cultural framework ...'.[38] In contrast to Marx, Winch is primarily concerned with understanding a different grammar rather than the possibilities of adopting a different grammar. None the less, his ideas are relevant to Marxism in so far as the unity of theory and practice suggests that an understanding of a different world-view is bound up with the struggle to attain that world-view. Of particular interest is the fact that Marxism has often been criticised for failing to provide guidelines and strategies for revolutionaries and for failing to delineate the communist *Weltanschauung*. Yet as Winch points out, 'the mere fact that we can find no application in our lives for a way of thinking which has an application in other cultural contexts is no good reason for arguing that it is "in principle impossible to understand" it'.[39] Whether or not an understanding would lead to its adoption is something that both Marx and Winch leave to history.

Generally, it is possible to 'translate' practices in Zande culture into terms intelligible in our own society. But the anthropologist does not merely have to learn what the Azande are doing when they consult their oracles, that is, the rules they are following. He must also learn *what it is* to consult the oracle, the meaning of that activity in that culture. Once again we confront the distinction between rules and grammar: we need to be able to grasp the grammar as well as the rules of an alien practice before we can be said to understand it or decide whether or not we could adopt it in our own culture. A humorous illustration of this may be found in Bob Newhart's hypothetical conversation with Walter Raleigh in which the latter is depicted as trying to persuade a contemporary to adopt the strange custom of smoking tobacco. This conversation demonstrates that a description of the rules of tobacco-smoking is insufficient to elucidate for others what that practice is, what people's reaction to it might be and its role in a particular culture.

The conclusion to be drawn is that if one wishes to introduce a new practice into a society one cannot simply make it intelligible by describing the rules which govern that practice. For the practice itself will only be immediately intelligible if the grammar of such a practice is already present in the society. For example, one may introduce new board games without difficulty precisely because people are already familiar with games. They know what a game is and have certain attitudes and reactions towards it, for example, they accept that it is played for fun and is not to be taken seriously, one does not shoot the loser and so on. Indeed new board games are introduced frequently and often they have a close relationship to particular social phenomena, as, for example, in the case of the game 'ulcers'. The notion of grammar, originally introduced by Wittgenstein and developed by later writers, may therefore be useful in understanding the nature of conceptual and social change. The limits of what can be said, the limits of social change, are determined neither by the natural objects nor by our ideas but by the relationship between them as expressed in the notion of grammar. Misled by the nebulous nature of the notion of grammar, many commentators have read a resemblance to conventionalism into Wittgenstein's rejection of an empirical realist ontology.

Wittgenstein's relationship to conventionalism

Confronted with the realist view, Wittgenstein exaggerates his conventionalism, presumably in order to throw into relief the difference between the two approaches. His account of the relationship between language and reality has led Dummett to describe his as a 'full-blooded conventionalist'. In his paper 'Wittgenstein's philosophy of mathematics', Dummett argues that for Wittgenstein:

> the logical necessity of any statement is always the *direct* expression of a linguistic convention. That a given statement is necessary consists always in our having expressly decided to treat that very statement as unassailable; it cannot rest on our having adopted certain other conventions which are found to involve our treating it so.[40]

In fact Wittgenstein explicitly rejects the view that our practices and ideas are simply a matter of arbitrary definitions. As he says in his *Remarks on the Foundations of Mathematics*:

> 'Then according to you everybody could continue the series as he likes; and so infer *any* how!' In that case we shan't call it 'continuing the series' and also presumably not 'inference'. And thinking and inferring (like counting) is of course bounded for us, not by an arbitrary definition, but by natural limits corresponding to the body of what can be called the role of thinking and inferring in our life.[41]

It would seem that here Wittgenstein is here jettisoning the notion of 'grammar' in favour of 'natural limits' but it should be remembered that he is using the expression 'natural' to refer to the nature of social life. The difference between his views and those of the conventionalists may be clarified by considering his account of inference given above. While the laws of inference may be determined by the role of inferring in social life, they do none the less possess as much power as if they were determined by the objects of the natural world. As Wittgenstein says:

> Nevertheless, the laws of inference can be said to compel us; in the same sense, that is to say, as other laws in human society. The clerk who infers ... *must* do it like that; he would be punished if he inferred differently. If you draw different conclusions you do indeed get into conflict, e.g. with society; and also with other practical consequences.[42]

Although they are simply a product of a particular society and possibly open to change, these laws are not to be taken lightly. One cannot simply decide to act differently as the conventionalists would argue. One cannot redefine these laws in isolation, since many other practices in our society hinge on the correct application of these laws. But while these inferences take their sense from their relationship to other practices they cannot be justified by reference to the nature of the world or experience as such. Wittgenstein makes a similar point in relation to calculation, which receives considerable attention in his later work:

> If I go over a calculation several times so as to be sure of having done it right, and if I then accept it as correct, – haven't I repeated an experiment so as to be sure that I shall tick the same way the next time? – But why should going over the calculation three times convince me that I shall tick the same way the fourth time? – I'd say: I went over the calculation 'so as to be sure of not having overlooked anything'.
>
> The danger here, I believe, is one of giving a justification of our procedure where there is no such thing as a justification and we ought simply to have said: *that's how we do it*.[43]

For there to be the practice of calculating there has to be agreement over what would count as the correct result of a calculation. The possibility of a different result must be *inconceivable* since our practice of calculating sets logical limits on what would constitute a correct result:

> Would it be possible that people should go through one of our calculations today and be satisfied with the conclusions, but to-morrow want to draw quite different conclusions, and other ones again on another day?
>
> Why isn't it imaginable that it should *regularly* happen like that: that when we make *this* transition one time, the next time, '*just for that reason*', we make a different one, and therefore (say) the next time the first one again? (As if in some language the colour which is called 'red' one time is for that reason called another name the next time, and 'red' again the next time after that and so on; people might find this natural. It might be called a need for variety.)[44]

> Isn't it like this: so long as one thinks it can't be otherwise, one draws logical conclusions. This presumably means: so long as *such-and-such is not brought in question at all.*
>
> The steps which are not brought in question are logical inferences. But the reason why they are not brought in question is not that they 'certainly correspond to the truth' – or something of the sort, – no, it is just that this is called 'thinking', 'speaking', 'inferring', 'arguing'. There is not any question at all here of some correspondence between what is said and reality; rather is logic *antecedent* to any such correspondence; in the same sense, that is, as that in which the establishment of a method of measurement is *antecedent* to the correctness or incorrectness of a statement of length.[45]

Wittgenstein can be distinguished from both the realist and the conventionalist. Although he maintains that the laws of inference are not determined by reality, he does not see them as completely arbitrary. Even though they are man-made constructions they none the less must be strictly adhered to if human activity is to continue.

Dummett's allegations concerning Wittgenstein's conventionalism have been criticised by Stroud in his paper, 'Wittgenstein and logical necessity'.[46] Here it is acknowledged that, given Wittgenstein's emphasis on linguistic conventions, the meanings of words and the rules for usage, it is difficult to distinguish his position from that of the conventionalists. Moreover, the conventionalist interpretation is strengthened by Wittgenstein's examples of possible alternatives to our system of calculating. For if Wittgenstein is reducing these differences simply to a difference in conventions, he would seem to be committed to a conventionalist position. This point hinges on whether the practices to which Wittgenstein draws attention are *conceivable* alternatives to our own. Stroud cites Wittgenstein's example of the tribe who measure wood rather differently from us, as an example of the alternative system of measurement:

> ... but what if they piled the timber in heaps of arbitrary, varying height and then sold it at a price proportionate to the area covered by the piles?
>
> And what if they even justified this with the words: 'of course, if you buy more timber, you must pay more'?[47]

Whilst this practice may seem intelligible in isolation – and even then it places a strain on the imagination – if considered in relation to other practices in that society its intelligibility is diminished. However, our inability to understand the practice and the role it has in that society merely reflects the limits our way of life imposes on our imagination rather than the limits of what is logically possible or meaningful. As Stroud says:

> Wittgenstein's examples are intended to oppose Platonism by showing that calculating, counting, inferring, and so forth, might have been done differently. But this implies no more than that the inhabitants of the earth might have engaged in those practices in accordance with rules which are different from those we actually follow. It is in that sense a contingent fact that calculating, inferring, and so forth, are carried out in the ways that they are – just as it is a contingent fact that there is such a thing as calculating or inferring at all. But we can understand and acknowledge the contingency of this fact, and hence the possibility of different ways of calculating, and so forth, without understanding what those different ways might have been. If so, then it does not follow that those rules by which calculating, and so forth, might have been carried out constitute a set of genuine alternatives open to us among which we could have chosen. The only sense that has been given to the claim that 'somebody may reply like a rational person and yet not be playing our game' is that there might have been different sorts of beings from us, that the inhabitants of the earth might have come to think and behave in ways different from their actual ones. But this does not imply that we are free to put whatever we like after '1000' when given the instructions 'Add 2', or that our deciding to put '1002' is what makes that the correct step. Consequently, Wittgenstein's examples do not commit him to a 'radical conventionalism' in Dummett's sense.[48]

Wittgenstein himself was well aware of this point: 'Nothing is more important for teaching us to understand the concepts we have than constructing fictitious ones'.[49] When he says that our calculations and inferences rest on judgements shared by a group, he does not mean that they are the products of free and spontaneous decisions. Of course they could be different, but in that case our entire way of life would be different since activity or practice sets limits to conventionalism, as Stroud has observed:

> The 'shared judgments' (for example, of sameness) upon which our being able to communicate rests, and which are responsible for our calculating, inferring, and so forth, as we do are not properly seen, then, as the results of free decisions in the manner of the logical positivists. They might have been different and, if they had been, then calculating, inferring, and so forth, would have been done differently. But this does not make them conventions in the positivists' sense ... These 'judgments' represent the limits of our knowledge ...[50]

We cannot justify our ways of calculating and inferring any more than we can justify our way of life or show it to be correct. Rather our way of calculating is given with our way of life. Dummett's claim therefore can be shown to be ungrounded. Wittgenstein's quasi-conventionalist approach can be seen as one more prong of his attack on the empirical realist ontology which avoids the arbitrariness usually associated with such a critique.

In rejecting an empirical realist position and emphasising social factors in the development of knowledge, it is not necessary to adopt a conventionalist standpoint, for the limits to conventionalism are provided by activity or praxis. This is expressed in Marx's strictures against the 'idealism' of the German philosophers and against contemplative philosophy in general. If one is simply a spectator rather than a participant in a society one can imagine a variety of conventions. But if one has to live with these conventions the situation is rather different. A conventionalist position therefore implies an essentially passive view of man. For the Hegelian-Marxists, like Wittgenstein, the focus instead is on the individual as an active member of society, holding certain values and beliefs derived from a specific historical situation. This emphasis on the interrelationship between theory and practice is the basic characteristic of Marxist thought. It is not the natural facts that set limits to the drawing up of new language-games or practices but the systems in which these facts are organised together with conventions, moral and political, that constitutes a limiting factor. Even outlandish ideas may be accepted as scientific provided that they have a point in relation to the beliefs and practices of people. Indeed, many of Wittgenstein's remarks on necessity stress the applicability of a convention rather than the facts as a limit to spontaneity.[51] The question of the primacy of nature and convention as expressed in the empirical realist and conventionalist arguments therefore loses its significance, as Pears has noted:

> There is something very academic about the fierce debate whether the sentence owes its necessary truth to the way things behave or to the way words behave, to nature or to convention. It would seem more sensible to say that neither of these two answers is quite adequate; rather, that the sentence is necessarily true because the words 'red' and 'green' pick out two classes which just do not overlap. One could say that this lack of overlap is the result of the way in which the two words are used, but since the two words pick out two classes of things, one could say equally well that it is the result of the nature of the things. Each of these two answers emphasises one aspect of the truth. But perhaps emphasis on either side is a mistake; perhaps the culprit is neither convention alone nor nature alone.[52]

The alternative to either nature or convention is to look at the role of particular ideas or practices in a system. Whilst Wittgenstein shares with the

Hegelian–Marxist tradition an emphasis on activity, he differs from this tradition in so far as he lacks an historical or political perspective and therefore never examines the social and political forces which govern the relationship between the individual and society. Consequently his work lends itself to a conservative interpretation, with the search for the limits to the adoption of a new world-view taking precedence over an exploration of the radical implications of his rejection of the empirical realist account of natural limits. While Wittgenstein's analysis of the relationship between nature and convention is valuable at an analytical level, we need to turn to Hegel and Marx for an historically and politically grounded transcendence of the nature–convention distinction.

Notes to Chapter V

[1] This chapter incorporates a revised version of an earlier paper, 'Conventionalism and the limits to social change', which appeared in *Social Praxis* (1979).

[2] K. Marx, *The Eighteenth Brumaire of Louis Bonaparte* (Moscow: Progress Publishers, 1967), p. 10; see also P. Winch, 'Authority', *Political Philosophy* ed. A. Quinton (Oxford: University Press, 1967), pp. 97–111.

[3] For a fuller account of conventionalism see L. Kolakowski, *Positivist Philosophy* (London: Pelican, 1972).

[4] H. Poincaré, *The Foundations of Science* (Lancaster, Pa.: Science Press, 1946); *Science and Hypothesis* (London: 1905); *Science and Method* (London: 1914).

[5] See E. Le Roy, *La Pensée Initiative* (Paris: 1929).

[6] In this sense Humpty Dumpty was a conventionalist although of course *Through the Looking Glass and what Alice Found There* (London, 1871) was written several years before Poincaré and Le Roy set out the rudiments of conventionalism.

[7] K. Popper, *The Logic of Scientific Discovery*, pp. 108.

[8] *Ibid.*, p. 108.

[9] It is for this reason that Popper sees Marxism as unscientific. *Conjectures and Refutations*, Ch. I.

[10] Popper's view that all basic statements cannot be challenged at the same time, for pragmatic reasons, contrasts with Wittgenstein's view that they cannot be challenged for *logical* reasons. For Wittgenstein, it is a condition of our being able to doubt that we take certain things for granted. From within the Marxist tradition Popper's decisionism has been criticised by Habermas in *Theory and Practice* (London: Heinemann, 1974). See J. Wisdom, *Challengeability in Modern Science* (Amersham: Avebury, 1982) for an attempt to extricate Popper from conventionalism.

[11] K. Popper, *The Open Society and its Enemies* (London: Routledge and Kegan Paul, 1945).

[12] See B. Williams, *Morality: An Introduction to Ethics* (Cambridge: University Press, 1972).

[13] See especially *On Certainty, Tractatus Logico-Philosophicus* and *Philosophical Investigations*; a good discussion of Wittgenstein's views in the later works is given in

E. K. Specht, *The Foundations of Wittgenstein's Late Philosophy* (Manchester: University Press, 1969).

[14] D. Pears, *Wittgenstein* (London: Fontana, 1971), p. 13.

[15] L. Wittgenstein, *Philosophical Investigations*, 43.

[16] Wittgenstein is here attacking Platonic realism. However Pears, *op. cit*., argues that Wittgenstein adopts a classical idealist position implying that our theories determine the objects we see. In fact Wittgenstein rejects both realism and idealism, arguing instead that our *practice* determines which objects we see.

[17] L. Wittgenstein, *Philosophical Investigations*, I, 11.

[18] *Ibid*., 360.

[19] *Ibid*., 23.

[20] P. Winch, 'Understanding a primitive society', *Ethics and Action* (London: Routledge and Kegan Paul, 1972), pp. 12–13.

[21] P. Winch, 'Language, belief and relativism', *Contemporary British Philosophy* fourth series, ed. H. O. Lewis (London: Allen and Unwin, 1976), p. 325.

[22] L. Wittgenstein, *Culture and Value* (Oxford: Basil Blackwell, 1980) p. 10e.

[23] P. Winch, 'Language, Belief and Relativism', p. 336.

[24] *Ibid*., p. 336.

[25] *Ibid*., p. 336.

[26] L. Wittgenstein, *Zettel* (Oxford: Basil Blackwell, 1967), 55. Wittgenstein's concept of grammar is born of a rejection of the contemplative philosophy of his earlier writings which generated problems of realism and solipsism. Wittgenstein transcends these problems in his later works by reference to praxis and in that sense moves closer to Marxism.

[27] L. Wittgenstein, *Remarks on the Foundations of Mathematics* (Oxford: Basil Blackwell, 1967), p. 30; *The Blue and Brown Books* (Oxford: Basil Blackwell, 1969), p. 56.

[28] Stuart C. Brown, *Do Religious Claims Make Sense?* (London: SCM Press, 1969), pp. 104–5.

[29] H. Schwyzer, in 'Rules and practices', *Philosophical Review* LXXVIII (1969), pp. 451–67 offers a critique of J. Searle, 'How to derive "ought" from "is"', *Philosophical Review* XXIII (1964); 'What is a speech act?', *Philosophy in America* (London: 1965), and of J. Rawls, 'Two concepts of rules', *Philosophical Review* LXIV (1955).

[30] H. Schwyzer, *op. cit*., pp. 464.

[31] S. Toulmin, *Human Understanding* I (Oxford: University Press, 1972); Stuart C. Brown, *op. cit*.

[32] S. C. Brown, *op. cit*., pp. 51–4.

[33] This point has been brought out well by A. MacIntyre in his paper 'Is understanding religion compatible with believing', in *Faith and the Philosophers* (London: Macmillan, 1964), where he points out that religious views cannot today be dismissed as mistaken. Rather they should be seen as hangovers from a way of life that has passed.

[34] S. C. Brown, *op. cit*., p. 104.

[35] L. Goldmann, *The Human Sciences and Philosophy* p. 123.

[36] P. Winch, 'Understanding a primitive society'.

[37] P. Winch, 'Language, belief and relativism', p. 330.

[38] *Ibid*., p. 330.

[39] *Ibid*., p. 330.

[40] M. Dummett, 'Wittgenstein's philosophy of mathematics', *Wittgenstein* ed. G. Pitcher (London: Macmillan, 1968), pp. 425–6.

[41] L. Wittgenstein, *Remarks on the Foundations of Mathematics*, Book I, 116.

[42] *Ibid.*,

[43] *Ibid.*, II, 74.

[44] *Ibid.*, I, 154.

[45] *Ibid.*, I, 155.

[46] B. Stroud, 'Wittgenstein and logical necessity', *Wittgenstein*, ed. G. Pitcher pp. 477–96.

[47] L. Wittgenstein, *Remarks on the Foundations of Mathematics*, I, 148.

[48] B. Stroud, *op. cit.*, pp. 489–90.

[49] L. Wittgenstein, *Culture and Value* (Oxford: Basil Blackwell, 1980), p. 74e.

[50] B. Stroud, *op. cit.*, p. 493.

[51] Wittgenstein, *Remarks on the Foundations of Mathematics* II, 8, 75; *Philosophical Investigations*, 120, 142, 542.

[52] D. Pears, 'Incompatibilities of colours', *Logic and Language* second series , ed. A. G. N. Flew (Oxford: Basil Blackwell, 1953), p. 112.

VI
The problem of relativism

A further problem raised by the notion of a world-view or world-picture is the problem of relativism which arises in the following ways: firstly, if our ideas are bound up with a particular form of life (Wittgenstein) or class position (Marx), how can we ever achieve objectivity? This problem is particularly acute if the theories of others are specifically denied objectivity on the basis of the intrusion of class interests. To avoid extreme relativism, we must find grounds for excluding some theories rather than others from the charge of subjectivity. We shall therefore examine the ways in which Marx and Mannheim exempt their own theories from the *tu quoque* charge. Secondly, when conflicting world-views clash with each other, how are we to evaluate the validity of those world-views? If the standards of rationality are internal to world-views or world-pictures, how may they be compared? This problem, raised by Wittgenstein in *On Certainty* is also of relevance to Marxists considering the conflict between different classes with their own distinctive world-views.

The tu quoque charge

Marxism is especially vulnerable to the *tu quoque* argument in so far as it equates ideology with modes of thought which further the interests of the ruling class. At the same time, Marxism advances ideas which claim to be scientific and correct, yet which champion the interests of the working class. But does this mean that it is effectively an ideology? If so, what are we to make of its claim to validity? If Marx's account of capitalist society is to be exempted from the *tu quoque* charge, what justification can we give for this exemption? Although Marx did not explicitly seek to provide an answer to these questions, we can discern in his work a possible solution, namely that the historical and social position occupied by the working class frees it from the distortion which plagues other classes, thereby endowing it with objectivity: 'the situation of the proletariat *brings it about* that its world-view, unlike that of any other class, is correct'.[1] Because it has the potential to develop an accurate understanding of the world, it can bring about a successful revolution. In equating the superior thought of the working class with its unique historical position, Marx anticipates Lukács who, as we saw earlier, contrasts bourgeois and proletarian consciousness in terms of the historical standpoint of the two classes.[2] Given that the world-view or world-picture embraces the form of life of the class, that form of life can be used as a source of validity for that world-view, in other words, the thought of the class is vindicated by its practice. This echoes Wittgenstein's theory of meaning: '*Practice*', he says, 'gives the words their sense'.[3] But we still need to establish which specific features of the working class's historical standpoint ensure objectivity. Lukács deals with this question in his essay 'The changing function of historical materialism', where he points to certain features of working-class life which distinguish it from all other classes.[4] Accepting that historical materialism must be applied to itself, he denies that this casts doubt on its validity:

> I believe that this objection can be upheld in part, but to concede it is not to the detriment of the scientific status of historical materialism. Historical materialism both can and must be applied to itself. But this must not be allowed to lead to total relativism, let alone to the conclusion that historical materialism is not the correct historical method.[5]

For Lukács the fact that historical materialism, as a social theory, is bound up with the aims and purposes of a class does not limit its claims to the truth. He offers two reasons to support this contention. First, he claims that historical materialism retains validity because it applies only to a particular society, namely capitalism. This claim is difficult to countenance, however, since Marx makes it clear that his theories apply to feudal and ancient modes of production as well as capitalism. As a theory of history, historical materialism must embrace earlier modes of production and their relationship to the present. Whilst his first argument is open to criticism, the second touches on an essential strand in Marxist thought. Lukács argues that ultimately Marxism can claim validity because at a certain stage of capitalist development, the interests of the working class coincide with the general interests of the human race. Because it is a universal class, with no particular interests to defend, it can achieve the total picture essential for objectivity. In portraying the working class as the universal class Marx is influenced by Hegel's *Philosophy of Right* which treats the bureaucracy as a universal class:

> But if Marx does not accept the Hegelian identification of bureaucracy with universality, he still retains the dialectical concept of a 'universal class', i.e. a partial social stratum which is, however, an ideal subject of the universal concept of the *Gemeinwesen*.[6]

The claim to universality, whether justified or not, is of significance since it is only by postulating its interests as the interests of all that a class can achieve and maintain power. As Marx says:

> No class of civil society can play this role without arousing a moment of enthusiasm in itself and in the masses, a moment in which it fraternises and merges with society in general, becomes confused with it and is perceived and acknowledged as its *general representative*; a moment in which its demands and rights are truly the rights and demands of society itself; a moment in which it is truly the social head and the social heart. Only in the name of the general rights of society can a particular class lay claim to general domination.[7]

> For each new class which puts itself in the place of one ruling before it is compelled, merely in order to carry through its aim, to present its interest as the common interest of all the members of society, that is, expressed in ideal form: it has to give its ideas the form of universality, and present them as the only rational, universally valid ones.[8]

A number of arguments designed to establish this universality have been advanced. Emphasis has been placed on the independence and autonomy of the working class in contrast to the dependence of all previous classes which have enlisted the support of other classes to ensure a successful revolution. This support has been won by advancing *particular* interests as universal ones, as epitomised by the slogans of the French Revolution, designed to rally support for the bourgeoisie from other classes.[9] But since there is no fundamental gulf between the interests of the proletariat and those of humanity, it is therefore not obliged to mask its interests, nor, given its strength of numbers, does it need the help of other classes. However, in recent years, movements for social change have drawn into the revolutionary arena a number of disparate classes. In Africa, for example, military coups have been effected, while in China and South-east Asia the revolutions have been peasant-based. The Russian revolution was seen by its architects as an alliance between intellectuals and workers although their interests may have diverged in practice. Possibly one could counter this by arguing that, precisely because of the *heterogeneity* of the revolutionary movement, it is able to arrive at a synthesis of various views and thereby effect a total understanding of social relations, but this would be closer to a Mannheimian than a Marxian perspective although Marx argues that with the polarisation of classes, increasing numbers of people are driven to the status of wage-labourers.[10] Regardless of their class origins, those groups with only their labour-power to sell effectively belong to the working class. However, the enormous expansion of the middle class during this century has cast some doubt on the thesis of polarisation although the recent trend towards unionisation among white-collar workers could be seen as an identification of their interests with the working class rather than owners of capital.[11] In most Western societies the gap between the two extremes of the social hierarchy is increasing and in this sense polarisation *has* occurred. Moreover, with the growth and consolidation of monopolies, the *petit-bourgeoisie* is finding itself in the position of sharing economic interests with the working class regardless of its perception of its own class interests.

The working class is also unique in the sense that in order to achieve emancipation it needs to destroy itself as a *class* while simultaneously destroying the class structure. Because it is propertyless it has no interests to defend, so in abolishing private property – the linchpin of the class structure – through its revolutionary praxis, it universalises its own condition and in emancipating itself also frees humanity:

> By proclaiming the *dissolution of the hitherto existing world order*, the proletariat merely states the *secret of its own existence*, for it *is in fact* the dissolution of that world order. By demanding the *negation of private property*, the proletariat merely raises to the rank of a *principle of society*, what society has made the principle of the *proletariat*, what, without its own co-operation, is already incorporated in *it* as the negative result of society.[12]

Once it achieves power, there will no longer be any classes left to challenge it, so it cannot become a declining class. This is significant since Marx often equates ideology and science respectively with the world-views of *declining* and *ascending* classes. Every class, at a certain stage in history, may claim to represent the general consciousness or will of society and may, for a limited period, have the power and support to justify this claim. But changing social conditions may render a gulf between the particular interests of a class and its general interests. We could therefore distinguish rising classes, 'those whose claims for universality represent at a given moment, the general will of society, and realize the potential of its development' from declining classes 'whose claim for universality is no longer valid and real'.[13] When this happens a class may start 'living in the past'. Indeed, the impression Marx often gave of the ruling class was of a class 'out of touch' with reality. In this context he distinguishes the thought of ascending and declining classes:

> The class making a revolution comes forward from the very start if only because it is opposed to a *class*, not as a class but as the representative of the whole of society, as the whole mass of society confronting the one ruling class. It can do this because initially its interest really is as yet mostly connected with the common interest of all other non-ruling classes, because under the pressure of hitherto existing conditions its interest has not yet been able to develop as the particular interest of a particular class.[14]

> This whole appearance, that the rule of a certain class is only the rule of certain

> ideas, comes to a natural end, of course, as soon as class rule in general ceases to be the form in which society is organised, that is to say, as soon as it is no longer necessary to represent a particular interest as general or the 'general interest' as ruling.[15]

Hence he often implied that political economy prior to the nineteenth century was scientific rather than ideological and expressed his admiration for Adam Smith.[16] During the period in which the bourgeoisie was rising to power, it was concerned to understand the economic principles underpinning the emerging capitalist society. But once the class established itself and began to fight off challenges to its supremacy, political economy degenerated into a form of ideology barely distinguishable from apologetics. By contrast, when the position of the working class is secure the challenge from other classes is no longer applicable, although Marx does not rule out the possibility of conflict in future communist society.

So far, the arguments we have considered stress the differences between the working class and other classes, but arguments for universality also rest on the identity of interests with the human species. Thus in his early work, Marx sees the working class as embodying the human essence in so far as it is a class of producers.[17] Since *homo sapiens* is *homo faber*, the interests of the working class cannot conflict with those of man. Its revolution does not constitute the revolt of a *class* as such, since it has no property and hence no class interests to defend, but is simply concerned with the fulfilment of its *species-being*. Its actions, in this sense, are taken on behalf of mankind. While it is arguable that the working class is not unique in this respect, since it shares its productive role with slaves, plebeians and serfs,[18] it differs from these subordinate classes in so far as it fulfils its project within a period of rapid industrialisation. With the development of trade, technological innovation, scientific knowledge and the intensification of the work process, Marx envisaged a decline in nationalism and the corresponding development of a genuine class consciousness which transcended national boundaries: in this sense the class was moving towards universality, for 'The working men have no country'.[19] One might argue that the resurgence of nationalism among the working class which has flourished throughout the twentieth century has somewhat retarded this process, but none the less recent developments show a move towards internationalism. The growth of multinational corporations, for example, has been matched by a corresponding increase in international co-operation between unions during industrial disputes. International solidarity during industrial disputes has manifested itself in the blacking of ships entering ports throughout the world. So the question of whether international class ties may supersede nationalistic sentiments is still pertinent today.

The idea of universality recurs in Marx's later work, particularly in *Capital*, where he ties universality to the specific historical conditions which shape the working class's *unique* position rather than in terms of its species-being as such, although the two notions are closely related.[20] He focuses his attention here on the commodity form, the *universal* form of modern capitalism. In so far as the worker is treated as a commodity, he experiences dehumanisation in its most extreme form. This dehumanisation is reflected in the fact that in capitalist society human relations appear as relations between things. Thus the alienation of the worker reflects the estrangement of humanity. The notions of reification and commodity fetishism are developed by Lukács who sees in the commodity form an identity between the subject and object of the historical process:

> The fate of the worker becomes the fate of society as a whole; indeed, this fate must become universal as otherwise industrialisation could not develop in this direction. For it depends on the emergence of the 'free' worker who is freely able to take his labour-power to market and offer it for sale as a commodity 'belonging' to him, a thing that he possesses'.[21]

Because its dehumanisation is so intense, the working class cannot sustain illusions about its condition. Its treatment as a commodity throws into relief the nature of capitalist social relations. This is problematic, however, since its dehumanisation is matched by its ability to find comfort in religious ideologies. Religion, as Marx observed, 'is the sigh of the oppressed creature, the heart of a heartless world, just as it is the spirit of spiritless conditions. It is the *opium* of the people'.[22] Pietism, for example, with its emphasis on self-renunciation, flourished among the impoverished classes after the Reformation. But Marx sees the emergence of Protestantism, in which the individual is divorced from the mediating intervention of the Church, as the appropriate form of religion for a society in which all relationships are reified. As he says in *Capital*:

> The religious world is but the reflex of the real world. And for a society based upon the production of commodities, in which the producers in general enter into social relations with one another by treating their products as commodities and values, whereby they reduce their individual private labour to the standard of homogenous human labour – for such a society, Christianity with its *cultus* of abstract man, more especially in its bourgeois developments, Protestantism, Deism, &c, is the most fitting form of religion.[23]

But where the working class shuns religious ideologies, its experience as a commodity places it in a unique position to grasp the relationships between different aspects of social life and thereby arrive at a total understanding of the world. Because of its extreme dehumanisation, it is forced to struggle against it whereas the capitalist, although alienated is, according to Marx, 'at home' in his alienation and not destroyed by it.

We can therefore identify a number of ways in which the working class can be seen as a universal class. Certain objections have been raised against this notion, mostly on the grounds of empirical or historical evidence, but as we have seen, these problems are not insurmountable. By referring to the universality of the working class, Marx is able to meet the *tu quoque* charge and to avoid the danger of lapsing into a Protagorean relativism. A similar argument is advanced by Mannheim who, following Hegel and Marx, saw a necessary relationship between the social structure of a group, the way it defines its political situation and the categories in terms of which experiences are organised.[24] By tying ideas to the social context, Mannheim exposes himself to the charge of relativism.

For if our ideas are limited by our changing forms of social life, how can we know if they have any validity? Indeed, Mannheim explicitly argues that those involved in the production process cannot see beyond their own interests. But if one accounts for ideas in terms of interests, does this mean that ideas have no autonomy? Moreover, given the 'limits to consciousness' exercised by the social milieu, how can we establish the correctness of Mannheim's own views on the subject? In dealing with the problem of relativism, Mannheim's solution is very similar to the Marxian treatment of this question. Both relate objectivity to the structural position of a particular group or class and both equate objectivity with a total grasp of social relations. But they differ in their choice of which group or class is to grasp the total picture and thereby achieve objectivity. Such a totalisation is to be achieved for Mannheim only by a group capable of transcending its particular interests and occupying a social position that is relatively classless. As he says:

> If it be once granted that political thought is always bound up with a position in the social order, it is only consistent to suppose that a tendency towards a total synthesis must be embodied in the will of some social group.[25]

Throughout history, he claims, this group has tended to be a 'marginal' one in the sense that it is open to attack from above and below, searching for an escape from its predicament. The total synthesis it achieves is not an aggregate of competing world-views but is a 'progressive development' drawing on the cultural heritage of previous ages. This demands an acute historical sensitivity and awareness of the dynamic nature of society and its unity, qualities suited to a stratum that occupies a marginal position in the social order. This stratum is composed of middle-class intellectuals who have a weaker class identification than those directly involved in the production process. They tend to come from a wide variety of backgrounds, being bound together only by their common educational experience. The class and status loyalties of the intellectual may not be completely eradicated, but:

> It is, however, peculiarly characteristic of this new basis of association that it preserves the multiplicity of the component elements in all their variety by creating a homogeneous medium within which the conflicting parties can measure their strength.[26]

For the intellectual is subject to:

> the influence of opposing tendencies in social reality, while the person who is not oriented toward the whole through his education, but rather participates directly in the social process of production, merely tends to absorb the *Weltanschauung* of that particular group and to act exclusively under the influence of the conditions imposed by his immediate social situation.[27]

Given this marginal position, intellectuals have tended either to join forces with one of the two antagonistic classes or to constitute a cohesive group of their own, in which case it is possible, as Mannheim says, that they 'will arrive at a consciousness – though not a class-consciousness – of their own general social position and of the problems and opportunities it involves'.[28] This consciousness places them in a better position than either workers or employers to achieve a broader grasp of social affairs and thereby achieve objectivity. It is in this way that he seeks to rescue his own theories from the *tu quoque* argument.

But objections to Mannheim's proposition may be raised: it is arguable that the intelligentsia, if it has not already joined forces with the ruling class, could construct an ideology shaped by its own interests, with group interests taking precedence over the desire for a total picture. Indeed, as Marx has argued, the intellectuals, far from being divorced from everyday political struggles, in fact serve the ruling class, legitimating the relationships of domination and subordination, although in times of revolutionary upheaval certain sections may join forces with the subordinate class. Given that bourgeois society had simplified class antagonisms, with 'Society as a whole ... splitting up into two great hostile camps, into two great classes directly facing each other: Bourgeoisie and Proletariat',[29] there is no room for a separate class of intellectuals in his analysis of capitalist society. However, speculation regarding the possible class sympathies of intellectuals does not necessarily invalidate Mannheim's claim regarding the *possibility* of a synthesis embodied in the unique historical experience of the intellectuals, any more than empirical evidence on the development of the class structure invalidates Marx's thesis regarding the universality of the working class. Both Marx and Mannheim thus seek to solve the problem of relativism by an appeal to the peculiar structural position of certain key groups, but they differ in their choice of groups endowed with objectivity. Whilst Mannheim held that the intellectuals were capable of transcending ideologies, Marx saw them as the creators and carriers of ideologies. Conversely, for Mannheim the working class was unable to grasp the totality because it was directly involved in the production process, while for Marx it was able to do so precisely because of its direct involvement in production.

Conflicting world-views

A further aspect of the problem of relativism is the difficulty of evaluating the nature of disagreements when world-views come into conflict. This problem has been considered by both Mannheim and Marx. In dealing with this question, Mannheim distinguishes between the particular and total conceptions of ideology. These two conceptions, he says, are used to study ideas in different ways. While the subject matter in each case is ideas, the particular conception is concerned with ideas which distort, namely, lies and deceptions, whereas the total conception is concerned in a broader sense with ideas characteristic of a particular age or class, that is, a world-vision or world-picture. In both cases we may encounter disagreement between the protagonists. But the disputes are dissimilar: in the case of the *particular* conception of ideology, protagonists of competing views can be said to share a common criterion of validity. For example, when we talk of lies and deceptions we are using a *particular* conception of ideology. As Mannheim says:

> The particular conception of ideology is implied when the term denotes that we are sceptical of the ideas and representations advanced by our opponent. They are regarded as more or less conscious disguises of the real nature of a situation, the true recognition of which would not be in accord with his interests. These distortions range all the way from conscious lies to half-conscious and unwitting disguises; from calculated attempts to dupe others to self-deception.[30]

The practice of lying presupposes a common criterion of validity. For example, a claim that all Irish people are thieves can easily be challenged by referring to crime statistics broken down into nationalities. In this case the disagreement takes place against a background of common agreement, including an agreement on what counts as a thief. This is not to say that human agreement is arbitrary but that it is a *presupposition* of there being a distinction between truth and falsity.

When Mannheim refers to ideology in the total sense he is talking of a situation in which agreement has broken down and where we can no longer even agree about what the issue is. In such cases there is no common ground.[31] Where we are dealing with competing world-views, we are referring to different standards of relevance which are internally related to those world-views. This is why arguments between, say, Christians and Marxists, fail to get off the ground. In conflicts falling within the total conception of ideology, the disputing parties do not share a common criterion of what would count as a settlement of the dispute. Particular judgements cannot be condemned as mistaken by their opponents since the whole world-view is seen as mistaken. Lacking a common criterion of relevance, the competing sides also lack the criterion to decide upon an appropriate course of action and, as Wittgenstein notes, ultimately denounce each other as foolish and heretical.[32]

Mannheim's account of the two kinds of disagreement has obvious parallels with the work of Wittgensteinians such as Beardsmore, who, in the following example, employs a similar argument to distinguish between an empirical and an ethical disagreement:

> Suppose, for instance, that someone tells me that Da Vinci's Mona Lisa has been moved to the Tate Gallery and I disagree. This would, I suppose, be a characteristic empirical disagreement; and the important thing to note is that, although it may be difficult to decide which of us is right, we can at least imagine what would solve the dispute. Though we may disagree in the judgments that we make, both of us agree about what would count as a reason for saying there was, or was not, a certain painting in the Tate. On the other hand, in ethical disputes nothing comparable need be true. Often these are not decidable, even in principle, simply because the disputants cannot even agree over what criteria to apply. They each have reasons for the judgments that they make, but neither admits the relevance of the other's reasons. The argument has reached deadlock.[33]

But although Beardsmore correctly points to the incommensurability of ethical disputes, he overestimates the extent of this incommensurability and thereby lapses into total relativism. Not all cases of moral disagreement necessarily lead to deadlock, for there may be various means of overcoming disagreement with only extreme cases leading to a complete impasse. A classic example of the kind of breakdown postulated by Beardsmore's use of the Wittgensteinian model is the clash between classes expressed in conflicts such as the Pilkington strike in 1970. One reason why the strike took so long to settle was that 'While each party had its own conception of what were the main issues, each also tended to refuse or even acknowledge the relevance of issues that were considered important to others. This essentially was what the prolonged strike was about and why it proved so hard to settle'.[34] Moral and political disagreement between classes is not stable but a constantly shifting situation which may on occasions erupt into conflict and breakdown, with deadlock resulting from confrontation between the two sides, while at other times, there may be sufficient common ground for understanding and agreement, with a *modus vivendi* being reached that may last for decades. Even in the extreme case of the conflict between workers and Cossacks during the Russian Revolution, the gulf between the two sides was momentarily bridged as we can see from the following example described by Trotsky:

> Cutting their way with the breasts of their horses, the officers first charged through the crowd. Behind them, filling the whole width of the Prospect, galloped the Cossacks. Decisive moment! But the horsemen, cautiously, in a long ribbon, rode through the corridor just made by the officers. 'Some of them smiled', Kayurov recalls, 'and one of them gave the workers a good wink'. This wink was not without meaning. The workers were emboldened with a friendly, not hostile, kind of assurance, and slightly infected the Cossacks with it. The one who winked found imitators. In spite of renewed efforts from the officers, the Cossacks, without openly breaking discipline, failed to force the crowd to disperse, but flowed through it in streams. This was repeated three or four times and brought the two sides even closer together. Individual Cossacks began to reply to the workers' questions and even to enter into momentary conversations with them. Of discipline there remained but a thin transparent shell that threatened to break through any second. The officers hastened to separate their patrol from the workers, and, abandoning the idea of dispersing them, lined the Cossacks out across the street as a barrier to prevent the demonstrators from getting to the centre. But even this did not help: standing stock-still in perfect discipline, the Cossacks did not hinder the workers from 'diving' under their horses. The revolution does not choose its paths: it made its first steps toward victory under the belly of a Cossack's horse.[35]

At a less dramatic level, an examination of strikes reveals a number of strategies, including negotiation and arbitration, which may be used to 'resolve' a conflict when deadlock occurs. 'The pressures against strike action', as Allen observes, 'can be seen most obviously when a national strike is called'.[36] Referring to the proposed railwaymen's strike in 1966, he describes the pressure from union leaders, management, the Cabinet and the media which eventually led to the calling off of the strike and concludes:

> Given the atmosphere in which the strike discussions took place it is remarkable that so many members of the N.U.R. executive maintained their resolve to strike for so long. In many other cases the resolve is dissipated soon after the initial impulse to act is passed. This is one important reason why most of the strikes which take place in Britain are those which are called spontaneously. Only if a strike is started while resentment is high can the effects of socialization be minimized. The longer the period between deciding to strike and starting it, the more effective are all the pressures against industrial action likely to be.[37]

Incommensurability, therefore, is not necessarily a permanent feature of moral/political conflicts since various tactics have been developed to deal with the conflicts at the heart of advanced capitalist societies. In this sense there is a limit to the relativism arising from the notion of a world-view. Furthermore, neither Wittgenstein nor Marx treat all world-views as fundamentally on a par with each other in terms of their respective merits. In his 'Remarks on Frazer's *Golden Bough*', for example, Wittgenstein is careful to distinguish between the significance and rightness of world-views:

> One could say 'every view has its charm', but that would be false. The correct thing to say is that every view is significant for the one who sees it as significant (but that does not mean, sees it other than it is). Indeed, in this sense, every view is equally significant.[38]

Similarly for Marx, as we noted earlier, each mode of production gives rise to its own appropriate principles, but this does not rule out the possibility of social criticism. Hence, in the Soweto example cited above, the two interpretations are of equal significance to those who hold them, but it does not follow that they are equally right. Bearing this in mind, we can see that the notion of a world-view offers an account of ideology which avoids extreme relativism.

Nor does the notion of a world-view commit Marxism to the élitism associated with the essence–appearance account of ideology. Some of the difficulties with this account have already been explored. On this view competing claims to the truth may be judged against reality and in this way Marxism is seen as the correct account. But the notion of an objective reality against which competing accounts may be judged is suspect since an objective truth is only intelligible within a world-view. The search for an underlying reality behind the phenomenal forms of social life has inevitably led to the kind of élitism expressed in the claim that 'There is, after all, some distance between the consciousness of even the most revolutionary worker and the science of Marx or Lenin'.[39] This élitism is far removed from Marx's stress on the need for the working classes to make their own revolution. Expressed in a letter in 1879:

> When the International was formed we expressly formulated the battle-cry: The emancipation of the working classes must be conquered by the working classes themselves. We cannot therefore co-operate with people who openly state that the workers are too uneducated to emancipate themselves and must be freed from above by philanthropic big bourgeois and petty bourgeois.[40]

The working class world-view for Marx is not validated by the ability of a particular section of society to possess an objective certitude that transcends all cultural and historical boundaries. A further difficulty with the notion of objective truth implied by the essence–appearance model is that it sees incommensurable views as essentially disagreements concerning the facts, and assumes that if the facts are supplied, disagreements may be resolved. For Marx world-views are, at times of crisis, incommensurable. In *Capital* he refers to crucial 'transitional' periods where conflicts erupt in revolution:

> In the history of primitive accumulation, all revolutions are epoch-making that act as levers for the capitalist class in course of formation; but, above all, those moments when great masses of men are suddenly and forcibly torn from their means of subsistence, and hurled as free and 'unattached' proletarians on the labour-market. The expropriation of the agricultural producer, of the peasant, from the soil, is the basis of the whole process. The history of this expropriation, in different countries, assumes different aspects, and runs through its various phases in different orders of succession, and at different periods. In England alone, which we take as our example, has it the classic form.[41]

He continues:

> As soon as this process of transformation has sufficiently decomposed the old society from top to bottom, as soon as the labourers are turned into proletarians, their means of labour into capital, as soon as the capitalist mode of production stands on its own feet, then the further socialisation of labour and further transformation of the land and other means of production into socially exploited and, therefore, common means of production, as well as the further expropriation of private proprietors, takes a new form. That which is now to be expropriated is no longer the labourer working for himself, but the capitalist exploiting many labourers. This expropriation is accomplished by the action of the immanent laws of capitalist production itself, by the centralisation of capital. One capitalist always kills many ... The monopoly of capital becomes a fetter upon the mode of production, which has sprung up and flourished along with, and under it. Centralisation of the means of production and socialisation of labour at last reach a point where they become incompatible with their capitalist integument. This integument is burst asunder. The knell of capitalist private property sounds. The expropriators are expropriated.[42]

Human disagreement of the kind encountered in clashes between different world-views which are, after all, clashes between different ways of life, traverse a wider area than factual discourse. Ultimately, the conflict between different world-views is overcome at times of extreme crisis, not by an appeal to facts but by a change in the way of life. The worker who familiarises himself with Marxism is therefore not simply coming to accept the truth of a set of claims but rather coming to accept new criteria for deciding on the truth of claims. What seemed adequate reasons for accepting claims on his earlier world view may no longer seem appropriate. The transition from one world-view to another rests upon a shift in the form of life. Ideas, on this model, are seen as internally generated by the world-view instead of imposed on them by an external agency possessed with theoretical knowledge.

Notes to Chapter VI

[1] G. A. Cohen, 'The workers and the word: why Marx had the right to think he was right', *Praxis* III–IV (Zagreb, 1968), p. 380.

[2] G. Lukács, 'Reification and the consciousness of the proletariat', *History and Class Consciousness*, pp. 83–222.

[3] L. Wittgenstein, *Culture and Value*, p. 85e.

[4] G. Lukács, 'The changing function of historical materialism', *History and Class-Consciousness*, pp. 223–55.

[5] *Ibid.*, p. 228.

[6] S. Avineri, *The Social and Political Thought of Karl Marx* (Cambridge: University Press, 1971), p. 57.

[7] K. Marx, 'Contribution to critique of Hegel's philosophy of law. Introduction', *Collected Works* III, p. 184.

[8] K. Marx and F. Engels, 'The German ideology', *Collected Works* V, p. 60.

[9] *Ibid.*

[10] K. Marx and F. Engels, 'Manifesto of the Communist Party', *Collected Works* VI.

[11] However, Marx had, in any case, acknowledged the importance of the middle classes, although he did not see their expansion as affecting the fundamental conflict of interest between owners of capital and sellers of labour power. Criticising Ricardo, he writes: 'What he forgets to emphasize is the constantly growing number of the middle classes, those who stand between the workman on the one hand and the capitalist and landlord on the other. The middle classes maintain themselves to an ever increasing extent directly out of revenue, they are a burden weighing heavily on the working base and increase the social security and power of the upper ten thousand'. *Theories of Surplus Value*, II (London: Lawrence and Wishart, 1969).
More recently, some of the difficulties in assessing this expansion have been aired by J. Westergaard and H. Resler in *Class in a Capitalist Society* (London: Pelican, 1976).

[12] K. Marx, 'Contribution to critique of Hegel's philosophy of law. Introduction', p. 187.

[13] S. Avineri, *op. cit.*, p. 58.

[14] K. Marx and F. Engels, 'The German ideology', pp. 60–1.

[15] *Ibid.*, p. 61.

[16] For a discussion of this point, see H. M. Drucker, *The Political Uses of Ideology* (London: Macmillan, 1974).

[17] K. Marx, 'Economic and philosophical manuscripts', *Collected Works* III; *Capital* I, Ch. 7, on the labour process.

[18] K. Marx and F. Engels, 'Manifesto of the Communist Party'.

[19] *Ibid.*, p. 502.

[20] K. Marx, *Capital* I, Ch. 1.

[21] G. Lukács, 'Reification and the consciousness of the proletariat', p. 91.

[22] K. Marx, 'Contribution to the critique of Hegel's philosophy of law. Introduction', p. 175.

[23] K. Marx, *Capital* I, p. 79.

[24] K. Mannheim, *Ideology and Utopia* (London: Routledge and Kegan Paul, 1960).

[25] *Ibid.*, p. 136.

[26] *Ibid.*, p. 138.

[27] *Ibid.*, p. 139.

[28] *Ibid.*, p. 143.

[29] K. Marx and F. Engels, 'The Manifesto of the Communist Party', p. 485.

[30] K. Mannheim, *op. cit.*, p. 49.

[31] A similar point is made by Wittgenstein when he says 'If a lion could talk, we could not understand him'. *Philosophical Investigations*, p. 223.

[32] L. Wittgenstein, *On Certainty*, 611.

[33] R. Beardsmore, *Moral Reasoning* (London: Routledge and Kegan Paul, 1969), p. x.

[34] T. Lane and K. Roberts, *Strike at Pilkingtons* (London: Fontana, 1971) p. 236.

[35] L. Trotsky, *The History of the Russian Revolution* I (London: Sphere Books, 1967), p. 112.

[36] V. Allen, *Militant Trade Unionism* (London: Merlin, 1966), p. 27.

[37] *Ibid.*, p. 29.

[38] L. Wittgenstein, 'Remarks on Frazer's *Golden Bough*', *Wittgenstein Sources and Perspectives* (Hassocks: Harvester Press, 1979), p. 71.

[39] N. Geras, 'Marx and the critique of political economy', *Ideology in Social Science*, ed. R. Blackburn, p. 302.

[40] K. Marx, 'Circular letter' (1879), *Selected Correspondence* (Moscow, no date).

[41] K. Marx, *Capital* I, p. 716.

[42] *Ibid.*, p. 763.

VII
Materialism and idealism

Although Wittgenstein's analysis of conflict and change resembles Marx's approach in a number of ways, as we have seen, none the less attempts have been made to polarise the two on the basis of the apparent idealism of the former which is contrasted with the materialism of the latter.[1] Thus Wittgenstein's remark that '*The limits of my language* mean the limits of my world' might be seen as an indication of his idealism.[2] But such an interpretation overlooks his remarks concerning the material and practical aspects of linguistic behaviour and his attempt to ground the notion of a world-picture in a specific mode of life from which it cannot be separated. Similarly, whilst Winch's emphasis on the concepts people hold has been seen as tantamount to a reduction of sociology to philosophy and in that sense as idealist, one can note that when analysing social relations in *The Idea of a Social Science*, Winch advocates a close study of the grammatical rules which people follow when engaging in social interaction.[3]

Attempts to locate Marx within the materialist tradition also meet with a number of difficulties. Marx has traditionally been seen as a materialist, albeit a dialectical or historical materialist, in sharp contrast to the idealist approach. But it is difficult to place him squarely in either of these categories, not least because the materialism–idealism distinction itself is open to criticism.[4] It is certainly difficult to find agreement among Marxists regarding the central characteristics of either materialism or idealism, beyond the vague assertion that the former accepts the primacy of matter whilst the latter stresses the primacy of consciousness. Furthermore, Marx himself uses the two terms in a number of different ways. Idealism is used firstly to refer to the specific philosophical doctrine associated with the Young Hegelians which focuses on ideas rather than existence, and secondly to philosophy in general, when he criticises its lack of concern with practical problems. Materialism is also treated somewhat ambiguously by Marx. Equating materialism on some occasions with the doctrine of the primacy of being, on other occasions he equates it with science. Marx clearly saw his own work as constituting a move away from philosophy or ideology towards science. Yet some of his remarks on philosophy suggest that he saw his own work as basically philosophical.

Grounds for a materialist interpretation of Marx may be found in his fervent condemnation of speculative philosophy in 'The German ideology' and 'The Holy Family'.[5] In the former, however, Marx and Engels seem to have exaggerated their materialism in order to distance themselves from the Young Hegelians. But at the same time, Marx draws attention to the dangers of a materialist philosophy which sees man as a mere product of material circumstances, deprived of any ability to change the world; and notes that 'the chief defect of all previous materialism – that of Feuerbach included – is that things (*Gegenstand*), reality, sensuousness are conceived only in the form of the *object*, or of *contemplation*, but not as *human sensuous activity, practice*, not subjectively'.[6] Such a materialism neglects any consideration of the powers of men which could bring about a change in social conditions and is therefore inherently conservative. It is no coincidence that Feuerbach himself failed to offer any critique of the appalling social conditions of his time, so when faced with 'a crowd of scrofulous, overworked and consumptive starvelings' he was forced 'to take refuge in the "higher perception" and in the ideal "compensation in the species", and thus to relapse into idealism at the very point where the communist materialist sees the necessity, and at the same time the condition, of a transformation both of industry and of the social structure'.[7] For Marx, this conservatism was a direct consequence of his method which focused on the 'sensuous world' of objects rather than the sensuous activity of individuals.

Just as Wittgenstein's 'linguistic idealism' is based on the production of language within a material context, so Marx's materialism locates material forces primarily in a social context and can therefore be distinguished from mechanistic materialism. While Feuerbach sees the objects of the material world as fixed and independent of human activity, for Marx, the objects of the sensuous world studied by the materialists are rather 'the product of industry and of the state of society': natural objects enter our world through the development of trade and commerce. He illustrates this with the example of the cherry tree which was 'only a few centuries ago transplanted by *commerce* into our zone, and therefore only *by* this action of a definite society in a definite age has it become "sensuous certainty" for Feuerbach'.[8] Marx here seems to be developing the Hegelian distinction between mediacy and immediacy which appears in Hegel's *Logic*:

> It is no less obvious that immediate *existence* is bound up with its mediation. The seed and the parents are immediate and initial existences in respect of the offspring which they generate. But the seed and the parents, though they exist and are therefore immediate, are yet in their turn generated: and the child, without prejudice to the mediation of its existence, is immediate, because it *is*. The fact that I am in Berlin, my immediate presence here, is mediated by my having made the journey hither.[9]

While we can see a shift in Feuerbach's work away from the realm of spirit or ideas to 'man': because he treats man as an 'object of the senses' he fails to make the shift from 'man' to 'men' essential to the Marxist method. As Marx notes, 'he never arrives at the actually existing active men, but stops at the abstraction "man"'.[10] In this sense materialism passes into its opposite, idealism: both seek to separate themselves from the world and both are inherently conservative. Marx contrasts the 'old materialism' of Feuerbach *et al.* with his own, which is predicated on 'social humanity'. Unlike the old materialists, Marx ties his materialism to practice and history and argues, as we noted earlier, that the individual cannot be seen as an abstraction, a point also stressed by Bukharin:

> Any empirical subject *always* goes beyond the bounds of 'pure' sensual 'raw material'; his experience, representing the result of the influence of the external world on the knowing subject in the process of his practice, stands on the shoulders of the experience of other people. In his 'I' there is *always* contained 'we'. In the pores of his sensations there already sit the products of *transmitted* knowledge (the external expressions of this are speech, language and conceptions adequate to words). In his *individual* experience there are included beforehand society, external nature and history – i.e. social history. Consequently, epistemological Robinson Crusoes are just as much out of place as Robinson Crusoes were in the 'atomistic' social science of the eighteenth century ... Of course, individual sensations are a fact. But historically, there is *no* absolutely unmixed individual sensation, beyond the influence of external nature, beyond the influence of other people, beyond the elements of mediated knowledge, beyond historical development, beyond the individual as the *product* of society – and society in active struggle against nature.[11]

At the same time Marx regards himself as a materialist in so far as he views his own work as a scientific account of social life rather than mere philosophising or ideologising. Sharing with Feuerbach a distrust of purely speculative approaches, Marx dismisses much of the thought of his contemporaries as unrigorous and unscientific. His anxieties concerning speculative philosophy emerge most clearly in his critique of the Young Hegelians whom, he claims, remain at the level of ideas rather than examining the material conditions of society. Whereas Marx sees alienation, for example, as resulting from and permeating social relationships and resolvable only by a radical change in those relationships involving the abolition of the division of labour and private property, the Young Hegelians reduce alienation to a state of consciousness. Marx sees such 'speculative idealism' as inimical to 'real humanism'.[12] Because philosophical criticism for the Young Hegelians was divorced from the practical concerns of everyday life, they inevitably saw emancipation as simply a matter of emancipating consciousness. Marx takes issue with this conception of philosophy in an article in the *Rheinische Zeitung*, where he tries to show that philosophy cannot be separated from social life. 'One can consult any history book', he comments, 'and find repeated with stereotyped fidelity the simplest rituals which unmistakably mark the penetration of philosophy into salons, priests' studies, editorial offices of newspapers and court antechambers, into the love and hate of contemporaries'.[13] Ultimately, Marx shares Hegel's conception of the relationship between the philosopher and his epoch, as we can see from the following remark:

> philosophers do not spring up like mushrooms out of the ground; they are products of their time, of their nations, whose most subtle, valuable and invisible juices flow in the ideas of philosophy. The same spirit that constructs railways with the hands of workers, constructs philosophical systems in the brains of philosophers. Philosophy does not exist outside the world, any more than the brain exists outside man because it is not situated in the stomach.[14]

In seeking to detach themselves from the real world, the Young Hegelians had departed from Hegel's conception of philosophy and it was left to Marx to restore the Hegelian unity between philosophy and the real. Thus, rejecting abstract distinctions between thought and being, Marx argues that 'Thinking and being are thus certainly *distinct*, but at the same time they are in *unity* with each other'.[15] To be sure, Marx argues that 'It is not the consciousness of men that determines their being but, on the contrary, their social being that determines their consciousness',[16] but an interest in being does not preclude an interest in consciousness. All it implies is that consciousness can be understood only in relation to social life, a point with which Winch and Wittgenstein would agree. Marx's emphasis on the primacy of social being is designed to contrast the views of the German idealists with his own. For the idealists, 'the starting-point is conciousness taken as the living individual', whereas for Marx 'it is the real living individuals themselves, and consciousness is considered solely as *their* consciousness'.[17] So when Marx argues that 'being determines consciousness' he is not describing a crude causal relationship in which ideas mirror social and economic life but rather grounding ideas in a broader framework, while still according them a degree of autonomy. In his own work he avoids the problem of assigning priority to either consciousness or being by focusing instead on practice.

Marx also considers the methodological implications of speculative philosophy which focuses on ideas at the expense of sociological analysis. He contrasts this with his own method in 'The German ideology' which takes as its starting-point 'real active man' and which sees 'The phantoms formed in the brains of men ... [as] necessarily, sublimates of their material life-process, which is empirically verifiable and bound to material premises'.[18] His antipathy towards speculative approaches re-emerges in the *Grundrisse* where he stresses the need for an empirical dialogue between concepts and evidence rather than relying on theory alone. He makes it clear that the task of theory is to elucidate the nature of reality in a conceptual form by examining the relationship between phenomena. While he accepts that theory, or the 'concrete totality', as he describes it, 'is ... in fact a product of thinking and comprehending', he denies that it is a product of the concept which 'generates itself outside or above observation and conception'.[19] Rather, he says, it is 'a product ... of the working-up of observation and conception into concepts'.[20] But while critical of the abstractions of his contemporaries, Marx does not underrate the importance of elaborating categories with which to understand the world, but insists that these categories are developed through observation and conception for 'in the theoretical method, too, the subject, society, must always be kept in mind as the presupposition'.[21] Critical of mindless empiricism with its blind dependence on the facts, Marx constructs his own social theory on the basis of categories such as class and value, arguing that:

> It seems to be correct to begin with the real and the concrete, with the real precondition, thus to begin, in economics, with e.g. the population, which is the foundation and the subject of the entire social act of production. However on closer examination this proves false. The population is an abstraction if I leave out, for example, the classes of which it is composed. These classes in turn are an empty phrase if I am not familiar with the elements on which they rest, e.g. wage labour, capital, etc.[22]

Marx rejects the method of the political economists who begin with the 'real' and then proceed towards 'ever thinnner abstractions',[23] in favour of a categorial approach which begins with simple relations such as 'labour, division of labour, need, exchange value', and moves 'to the level of the state, exchange between nations and the world-market'[24] which he describes as 'obviously the scientifically correct method'. He elaborates, in typically Hegelian language:

> The concrete is concrete because it is the concentration of many determinations, hence the unity of the diverse. It appears in the process of thinking, therefore as a process of concentration as a result, not as a point of departure, even though it is the point of departure in reality and hence also the point of departure for observation (*Anschauung*) and conception.[25]

Using this method, we arrive at a fuller understanding of the social totality, for 'abstract determinations lead towards a reproduction of the concrete by way of thought'.[26]

Certain aspects of Marx's work therefore distinguish him from speculative philosophy and Feuerbachian materialism which he sees as essentially ahistorical. In its place Marx, like Wittgenstein, offers a practical approach. Just as Marx sees philosophy and religion as the product of the separation of mental and manual labour, so Wittgenstein describes philosophy as arising from the 'idling of language'.[27] Marx compares the relationship between philosophy and the world to the relationship between 'onanism and sexual love', while Wittgenstein saw philosophy as language broken loose from its moorings, sharing with Marx the view that philosophy could be disposed of by a return to meaningful activity. But this philosophical looseness was not seen by either as arbitrarily related to human practices nor as a product of linguistic confusion. Whilst critical of the abstract issues raised by the Young Hegelians, Marx was fully aware that they bore some relationship to the life they reflected. Marx clearly saw German philosophy as 'a consequence of German petty-bourgeois conditions'.[28] He continues:

> The philosophers have only to dissolve their language into the ordinary language, from which it is abstracted, in order to recognise it as the distorted language of the actual world, and to realise that neither thoughts nor language in themselves form a realm of their own, that they are only *manifestations* of actual life.[29]

Speculative philosophy could be seen as expressing the withdrawal of intellectuals from public life during the period of upheaval culminating in the 1848 revolution and, at a deeper level, the separation of mental and manual labour which could be transcended only by the abolition of the division of labour. Consequently a solution to philosophical problems for Marx and Wittgenstein lay in the realm of practice. But while Wittgenstein's solution to the idling of language lay in a return to *ordinary* practice, Marx sought to replace philosophy with *revolutionary* practice. Recognising that philosophy has its origins and solutions in practical life, Marx's importance lay in showing how, and under what circumstances, ideas and actions could be separated.

So although Marx is critical of *speculative* philosophy, he does not see all philosophy as irrelevant but rather as 'the living soul of culture'.[30] Philosophy, for both Marx and Wittgenstein, is a liberating activity. For Marx, critical philosophy was of crucial importance in subverting the *status quo* and in the hands of the proletariat, it is transformed into a powerful weapon:

> As philosophy finds its *material* weapons in the proletariat, so the proletariat finds its *spiritual* weapons in philosophy ... The *emancipation of the German* is the *emancipation* of the *human* being. The *head* of this emancipation is *philosophy*, its *heart* is the *proletariat*. Philosophy cannot be made a reality without the abolition of the proletariat, the proletariat cannot be abolished without philosophy being made a reality.[31]

He constantly emphasises that philosophy can only be transcended by making it real, for 'when the reality is described, a self-sufficient philosophy (*die selbständige Philosophie*) loses its medium of existence'.[32] Similarly for Wittgenstein, philosophy frees us from our bewitchment by language: the end of philosophy is to be found in a return to human practices as reflected in everyday language.

Given the importance Marx attaches both to a categorial approach *and* to the grounding of his method in the study of social relationships, it is difficult to identify him as either a materialist or idealist. Although idealists and materialists are often treated by contemporary philosophers as constituting two distinct species, they share, as Marx notes, a lack of interest in the everyday affairs of social life. In focusing upon practice, however, Marx transcends the distinction between the material and the ideal. Whilst it is crucial to his analysis that the individual creates his world through social activity, this does not preclude the use of categories such as labour when seeking to understand experience. His emphasis on categories is matched by an overriding concern with the practical nature of everyday life: when analysing the concept of alienation, for example, he arrives at the conclusion that alienation can be eliminated only through a radical change in social relationships rather than merely conceptual investigations. A sharp distinction between materialism and idealism also tends to assume a gulf between economics and philosophy which is alien to Marx. Although the dialectical materialists of the 1920s and 1930s concentrated on Marx's economic theories rather than his philosophical approach, since the discovery of the 'Paris manuscripts' socialist humanists, using categories such as alienation and reification, have shown that economics and philosophy are not logically exclusive in Marx's work, that his insights into the economic structure are in fact predicated upon certain philosophical assumptions regarding human activity. Essential to contemporary critical theory is the ability to erect a critique of social life on a sophisticated philosophical basis.

But in transcending the materialism–idealism distinction, Marx in fact moves closer to the classical German idealists than he would have acknowledged, since he seems at times to have equated the ideas of Hegel and the classical idealists with the inferior speculations of their successors. For the classical idealists also try to overcome this false dichotomy: in Fichte's 'critical idealism', for example, we find elements of both a materialist and an idealist approach: it is materialist in the sense that it accepts the independence and reality of the world but idealist in so far as it constitutes a highly speculative categorial analysis.[33] Like the classical idealists, Marx respects philosophical thought which he sees as expressing the human striving for knowledge essential to the transformation of the world. Following Hegel, he seeks to relate metaphysical categories to particular stages of historical development. If Marx can be shown to reject a crude materialist thesis and to be part of the German philosophical tradition rather than radically opposed to it, then no insuperable barrier exists to prevent a reconciliation between Wittgenstein and Marx. However, it has been argued that the conservatism implicit in a Wittgensteinian social science sets it apart from Marxism and it is this problem which we shall now consider.

Notes to Chapter VII

[1] Lenin's *Materialism and Empirio-Criticism* might be seen as an extreme form of materialism within Marxism while the affinity of the Wittgensteinians with idealism has been noted by Manser: 'there is a contemporary view which can be made to look very like idealism in the Hegelian sense, particularly if one realises that the substitution of "language" for "consciousness" or "mind" does not solve or dissolve problems but only transfers them into a new realm. I am referring to that form of Wittgenstein's philosophy which is espoused by what might be called the "Swansea group". The point here is that the "external world" is seen as mediated through our language. It is obvious that we cannot talk about the world without using language. But if you follow this line to its logical conclusion then the structure of the external world is something which is imposed by us' (A. R. Manser, *Marx and Philosophy*, unpublished ms.).

[2] L. Wittgenstein, *Tractatus Logico-Philosophicus* (London: Routledge and Kegan Paul, 1961), 5. 6.

[3] P. Winch, *The Idea of a Social Science and its Relation to Philosophy* (London: Routledge and Kegan Paul, 1958).

[4] See, for example, T. Rockmore, 'Fichte's idealism and Marx's materialism', *Man and World*, VIII, (May 1975), pp. 189–206.

[5] K. Marx and F. Engels, 'The Holy Family', *Collected Works* IV; 'The German ideology', *Collected Works* V.

[6] K. Marx, 'First thesis on Feuerbach', *Collected Works* V, p. 6.

[7] K. Marx and F. Engels, 'The German ideology', p. 41.

[8] *Ibid.*, p. 39.

[9] G. W. F. Hegel, *The Logic of Hegel*, trans. W. Wallace, p. 130.

[10] K. Marx and F. Engels, 'The German ideology', p. 41.

[11] N. I. Bukharin, 'Theory and practice from the standpoint of dialectical materialism', pp. 12–13.

[12] K. Marx and F. Engels, foreword to 'The Holy Family', p. 7.

[13] K. Marx, article in *Rheinische Zeitung*, (10 July 1942), *Collected Works* I, pp. 195–6.

[14] *Ibid.*, p. 195.

[15] K. Marx, 'Economic and philosophical manuscripts', *Collected Works* III, p. 299.

[16] K. Marx, 'Preface to contribution to critique of political economy', *Marx and Engels Selected Works* I (Moscow: Foreign Languages Publishing House, 1962), p. 363.

[17] K. Marx and F. Engels, 'The German ideology', p. 37.
[18] *Ibid.*, p. 36.
[19] K. Marx, *Grundrisse*, p. 101.
[20] *Ibid.*, p. 101.
[21] *Ibid.*, p. 102.
[22] *Ibid.*, p. 100.
[23] *Ibid.*, p. 100.
[24] *Ibid.*, p. 100–1.
[25] *Ibid.*, p. 101.
[26] *Ibid.*, p. 101.
[27] L. Wittgenstein, *Philosophical Investigations*, 38, 132.
[28] K. Marx and F. Engels, 'The German ideology', p. 447.
[29] *Ibid.*, p. 447.
[30] K. Marx, *Rheinische Zeitung*, (10 July 1942), p. 195.
[31] K. Marx, 'Contribution to critique of Hegel's philosophy of law', *Collected Works* III, p. 187.
[32] K. Marx and F. Engels, 'The German ideology', p. 37.
[33] This point is made by T. Rockmore, *op. cit.*

VIII
Marx and Wittgenstein

An alignment between Marx and Wittgenstein may seem implausible, given that Wittgenstein did not see himself as concerned in any way with social research. On the whole little attempt has been made by Wittgenstein's disciples to relate his ideas to the social sciences. One notable exception is, of course, Winch who has endeavoured to rework Wittgenstein's ideas into a programme for the social sciences,[1] but even his social philosophy has been seen as inimical to Marxism. Although Marxism and Wittgensteinian social philosophy may seem unlikely bedfellows, the possibility of a reconciliation between them will now be considered. In recent discussions of this question, a number of possible points of convergence have been identified.[2] Benton, for example, argues that the distinction between depth and surface grammar in Wittgenstein's work could be given a Marxian sense by applying it to investigations of social life. He draws a parallel between the notions of depth and surface grammar and real and phenomenal forms. On his account, the true relations of capitalist society are reflected in the depth grammar which is, for the majority of people, concealed by the various forms of surface grammar, that is, the phenomenal forms of capitalist society (see Chapter II). Social science goes beyond the unreflective account people give of their lives and arrives at a true account of social life. In Wittgenstein's work, Benton thus seeks the basis of a 'social-science methodology of ideological exposure'.[3] However, he distinguishes sharply between the work of Wittgenstein and Winch, arguing that although Winch's thought is inherently conservative, for reasons we shall consider in due course, Wittgenstein's work can provide much of interest to followers of Marx. While it is extremely doubtful that Wittgenstein ever conceived of the role of the philosopher as a 'super-scientific' one in the way in which Benton implies, he does rightly emphasise the radical nature of Wittgenstein's attempt to marshal the energy of philosophers against the bewitchment of our intellect in a way that the 'bourgeois Wittgenstein' of Winch's text does not and shows that Wittgenstein possessed rather more interest in the kinds of problems Marx was dealing with than Winch's work suggests.[4] But while the relationship of Wittgenstein to his disciples is problematic, nevertheless it will be argued here that there is nothing in Winch's work *per se* that rules out the possibility of a Marxian approach to the understanding of social life.

In establishing this point we shall encounter a number of criticisms of Wittgensteinian philosophy which, if justified, would drive a wedge between Wittgenstein and Marx. As we shall see, many modern social philosophers – not necessarily Marxists – have taken issue with certain features of Wittgensteinian social philosophy which apparently rule out the applicability of the Marxian notions of ideology and false consciousness. Three aspects of this quasi-Marxist critique can be identified. Firstly, Winch assumes that the account people give of their lives is unambiguous and not in need of correction or enlightenment on the part of the social theorist. Consequently, it is argued that he cannot allow for the fact that people may in some sense be mistaken about social life, that is, he does not allow for ideology. Secondly, his reliance on 'internal' explanations and his respect for tradition could be seen as inherently conservative. Thirdly, his emphasis on particular rather than universal standards suggests a relativist position.

The Marxist critique of Wittgenstein

(a) *Consensus and conflict*

'According to Winch', says MacIntyre, 'the successful sociologist has simply learned all that the ideal native informant could tell him; sociological knowledge is the kind of knowledge possessed in implicit and partial form by the members of a society rendered explicit and complete'.[5] In elucidating a form of life, the sociologist must offer explanations which are intelligible in terms of the concepts of the people being studied; if he wishes to go beyond these conceptions, his account must at least presuppose an initial understanding and be translatable into those concepts. This emphasis on 'internal explanation' lies at the heart of the debate concerning Winch's contribution to methodology. In contrast to Winch, Marx offers an account of capitalist society which differs radically from that of the 'native informant'. As Marx says:

> Just as our opinion of an individual is not based on what he thinks of himself so can we not judge of such a period of transformation by its own consciousness; on the contrary, this consciousness must rather be explained from the contradictions of material life, from the existing conflict between the social forces of production and the relations of production.[6]

In giving social explanations, Marx therefore uses concepts such as 'reification' and 'alienation' which may be unfamiliar to the people being studied. For Marx the 'native informant' possesses an inadequate knowledge of social life. It is, therefore, unnecessary for the social theorist to take his views into consideration or to couch his explanation in terms intelligible to him. This would seem to suggest a basic difference between Winch and Marx.

But does Winch accept that the native informant is infallible? In an unpublished reply to MacIntyre he denies the charge that he accepts the native informant's view as *necessarily* correct: there is no more reason to expect the native informant to give a clear account of his ideas and actions than to expect a contemporary Englishman to explain what he means by thinking.[7] Winch tries to meet MacIntyre's – and the hypothetical Marxist's – objection by pointing out that not all features of social life may be transparent to the members, and it is consequently quite possible for the native informant to be mistaken. Winch also allows that diverse and conflicting accounts of social life may exist. MacIntyre's claim that Winch holds what might be called a consensus view of social life is therefore avidly denied by Winch.

MacIntyre also claims that Winch rules out the possibility of ideology, for his emphasis on rule-following obliterates the distinction between what people claim to do and what they actually do. Yet the rules people claim to follow, says MacIntyre, may in fact be unrelated to the rules which actually govern their actions. Furthermore, Winch's assumption that ideas and actions are internally related implies that men cannot act in ways that are contrary to beliefs, that there cannot be a split between ideas and practices. Yet for many Marxists the notion of ideology rests on such a gulf. Even for non-Marxist sociologists the discrepancy between ideas and actions provides a fruitful area for social research. It has been shown, for example, that many people engage in petty pilfering even though they are committed to a moral imperative against stealing.[8] Such pilfering may be condoned because 'the goods won't be missed', '*they* can afford it', 'everyone does it' and so on. This indicates a contingent or external relationship between ideas and reality which is apparently inexplicable on Winch's account. In reply to this charge, Winch denies that his emphasis on rule-governed behaviour precludes a distinction between rule-acknowledged and actual behaviour.[9] He also concedes that people can be mistaken about ideas and social life – entailing a divergence between ideas and practice – but maintains that at a deeper level there is an identity between the two in the sense that ideas do not exist in a vacuum. But this does not prevent us from holding conflicting beliefs regarding certain actions, as in the example of pilfering. To hold that ideas are internally related, in the sense that actions express ideas, does not rule out the possibility of people engaging in acts which conform to some ideas but not others.

A more penetrating criticism of Winch is that he rules out the use of the *concept* of ideology as a means of explaining mistaken or contradictory beliefs, for to invoke this concept when giving social explanations presupposes a criterion of rationality external to particular societies, which Winch would reject. This criticism is made by Benton who claims that in excluding the notion of ideology Winch rules out the possibility of a critical or emancipatory social science. Yet Winch can meet this criticism: there is nothing, he says, to prevent us from making the concept of ideology intelligible to the people we are studying, but to do so, we must tie it to the concepts that they already possess. When invoking the concept of ideology we need to be clear regarding the sense in which we are using it. If we use it to refer to a separation between ideas and practices, to distorted beliefs which are distorted because they do not accurately reflect the practices of actual societies, then it is up to the observer to relate this notion to the concepts of the people concerned, pointing out to them the ways in which he believes their ideas to be mistaken. Similarly, concepts like reification and alienation, essential to Marxian social theory, can be tied to the concepts of the people under consideration. That wage labour is alienated labour, that the worker is treated as a commodity, is certainly not beyond the grasp of the factory worker. Indeed it is arguable that he knows the meaning of such terms better than the Marxist theoreticians. On the other hand, whilst the agents of actions may be the best source of authority for the reasons for their actions, it does not follow that they are infallible. An outsider can clarify their actions by contrasting the agent's account with the practices of the society and thereby provide a major insight into the workings of the society. What must be conceded to Winch, however, is that in explaining such a discrepancy between ideas and practice, the concepts of the people concerned play a crucial role in our explanation.

(b) *Conservatism*

Winch has also been seen as conservative in so far as he favours explanations in terms of reasons rather than causes, for in excluding causal explanations, argues MacIntyre, Winch rules out the possibility of constraining and repressive relationships.[10] MacIntyre contrasts Winch's work with that of Goffman whose work on total institutions shows the constraining effects institutions may have on people's ideas and actions.[11] But Winch claims that he does not rule out constraint *a priori* simply because he rejects the applicability of causal relationships.[12] Constraint, as he rightly points out, is intelligible even when causal language is inappropriate. He gives the example of the power a domineering mother has over her son. In analysing this relationship and demonstrating to the son the reasons for his actions, we do not need to refer to external causes. All we need to do is to make him see the relationship between himself and his mother in a new light. In analysing the reasons for actions, we are therefore just as likely to identify constraint as those who rely on causal accounts.

Further evidence of Wittgensteinian conservatism may be sought in Winch's argument that certain practices cannot be criticised from outside that way of life.[13] But whilst Winch's remarks on criticism contrast sharply with Marx's critique of bourgeois society, Marx in fact shares with Winch the essentially Wittgensteinian view that a standard of criticism must be internal to a mode of production or way of life. The fundamental difference is that Marx emphasises *conflicting* standards within a mode of production or way of life and is prepared to ally himself with one of them. Even within a specific mode of production, standards exist by means of which that way of life may be criticised. What may appear as an external standard is for Marx an internal one since it arises within capitalist society. It is in this sense that Marx emphasises that capitalism contains within itself the seeds of its own destruction.[14] Whilst capitalism gives us the framework in terms of which to understand it, it also engenders the categories which enable it to be criticised and creates the class which is to use those categories as an initial stage in transcending that society.

Neither Winch nor Marx in fact reject the legitimacy of criticism – they only question the legitimacy of certain *kinds* of criticism. For Winch, certain criticisms are incorrect because they are based on a mistaken idea of *what* is being criticised.[15] To see Zande magical practices as akin to scientific institutions in Western society and to criticise the former from the standpoint of the latter is one example given by Winch. Earlier anthropologists, under the sway of positivism, with its reverence for science, had often treated magical practices as a primitive form of scientific understanding. Such an account, argues Winch, rests on a basic misunderstanding, for in talking of magical beliefs we are not referring to hypotheses open to testing and falsification. Acceptance of witchcraft does not imply an acceptance of beliefs concerning the particular powers of particular people but rather refers to a basic feature of that way of life. Of course the beliefs of the Azande conflict with the findings of Western science but interpretations of those beliefs as 'primitive science' fail to capture the meaning of witchcraft in that society. While there is scepticism within Zande society concerning the power of witches, these sceptics do not doubt that there are such things as witches. In fact to talk of 'a belief in witches' can be misleading since we are dealing not just with a set of beliefs but with the whole way of life of the society.

Winch is here following the line of argument advanced by Wittgenstein in his 'Remarks on Frazer's *Golden Bough*', where he claims that it is mistaken to analyse a primitive practice from an external standpoint and to then conclude that it is based upon an error:

> The very idea of wanting to explain a practice – for example, the killing of the priest–king – seems wrong to me. All that Frazer does is to make them plausible to people who think as he does. It is very remarkable that in the final analysis all these practices are presented as, so to speak, pieces of stupidity.
>
> But it will never be plausible to say that mankind does all that out of sheer stupidity.
>
> When, for example, he explains to us that the king must be killed in his prime, because the savages believe that otherwise his soul would not be kept fresh, all one can say is: where that practice and these views occur together, the practice does not spring from the view, but they are both just there.[16]

When studying a primitive religious practice, we cannot advance our understanding by the use of Western concepts, 'one can only *describe* and say: this is what human life is like'.[17] For Wittgenstein, 'Frazer is much more savage than most of his savages, for they are not as far removed from the understanding of a spiritual matter as a twentieth-century Englishman. *His* explanations of primitive practices are much cruder than the meaning of these practices themselves'.[18] Similar problems arise in understanding religious practices in our own society. From a Wittgensteinian standpoint, it would constitute a misunderstanding to argue against religion on the grounds that empirical proof of God's existence is lacking, for to do so would be to miss the point of religion. Theologians have offered empirical proofs but this evidence is inconclusive to both the converted and the unconverted. Even the converted, when confronted with the same set of facts, may arrive at very different conclusions. Jehovah's Witnesses, for example, point to natural disasters as proof of God's wrath and *ergo* of God's existence. Conversely, a Catholic might refer to the wonders of life as evidence of a very different kind of God. But ultimately such empirical evidence is not decisive. Hence we can observe the scepticism which usually accompanies the apparent 'miracles' happening at Lourdes. People continue to believe when faced with lack of evidence and reject beliefs even when confronted with proof.[19] Practitioners of religion are not concerned with whether their beliefs can be empirically proven but with living their lives in accordance with certain precepts or values.

In giving a social explanation of religion, therefore, Marx never engages in theological arguments. Instead of examining the validity of religious beliefs, he instead reflects on the role of religion in social life, seeing it as a form of alienation expressing specific social relationships. Like Winch, Marx is not concerned to refute religion or to compare religion with science but rather to grasp what religion *means* within a particular way of life. Their point of difference is not over the facts as such but over the *meaning* of the practice to those concerned. For Winch, religion reflects something which he expresses vaguely as 'deep' in human life. For Marx, religion is a form of alienation which is a basic feature of capitalist society rather than of human activity as such. It, follows, therefore that the need for religion will be transcended with the supersession of capitalist society. But to say this is not to undervalue the importance that religion does have for people or to dismiss it as merely illusory. Suspicions of Winchean conservatism cannot therefore be wholly endorsed by an appeal to Winch's rejection of criticism, since Winch is concerned only to show that a critique which appeals to scientific rationality is misguided.

(c) *Relativism*

Closely bound up with the attack on Winchean conservatism is the attack on his 'relativism'. This is hardly surprising, since Winch's respect for tradition and his reluctance to criticise existing practices seem to commit him to a relativist position. Conversely, it is because Winch rejects the idea of an external standard of rationality that he has no truck with critiques of religion from the standpoint of Western science. Winch's point that the criteria of logic and rationality are embedded in particular ways of life, within particular language-games, has found many critics who object to the implicit denial of a superior or external measure against which different ways of life may be judged.[20] Gellner, for example, sees Winch's denial as an unwarranted assertion of the equality of cognitive powers. 'No one', he says, 'least of all those who are deprived of it, has any doubts about the superior cognitive effectiveness of the "scientific outlook".'[21] Likewise, no one doubts the inferiority of pre-scientific views. To see the two outlooks as equal is unrealistic and conflicts with the actual practice of societies. Gellner then accuses Winch of 'endorsing witchcraft and oracles'. According to Gellner, Winch's alleged neutrality regarding the rationality of magical practice is in fact a camouflage for a romantic traditionalism. Moreover, in ruling out the existence of an external standard of rationality he is committed to a relativist position.

One difficulty with Gellner's position is that it is by no means clear that the modern scientific outlook and the society it has engendered are superior. For Gellner its value lies in its ability to satisfy human needs. In a purely utilitarian sense a technological society delivers the goods, or at least has the potential to do so, by eliminating repetitive work and allowing for the full development of cultural and artistic sensibilities, yet this advantage must be set against the obvious disadvantages of technological societies such as pollution. Indeed, the crude equation of socialism with technology has long since been abandoned by Marxists. The Marxian critique of technological rationality lends support to Winch's view that the standards of social assessment do not have to come from scientific progress.[22] This scepticism regarding technology reveals a further possible point of contact between Wittgensteinians and humanist Marxists.

Of course Gellner could argue that the problems of technological society result from the *misuse* of technology. Science can provide a superior knowledge of empirical facts; it therefore has the potential to provide a better way of life. Certainly there can be no doubt that science does provide a specialised and systematic knowledge undreamt of by earlier generations. But for all that it is still only one way, among many, of making the world intelligible. A scientific explanation of disasters, for example, exists alongside the Jehovah's Witnesses' account. The two views, however, do not compete with each other since they belong to different language-games and fulfil different aims. The former provides simply a technical explanation of a natural event while the latter consolidates religious beliefs and gives meaning and expression to those beliefs. Indeed the two are compatible in the sense that one could accept a scientific account of the natural world and yet still hold, say, that the world reflects God's glory.

Precisely because the language-games of science and magic or religion are not in competition with each other, Winch does not feel it necessary to compare them or 'rate' them according to scientific criteria. For him it does not even make sense to ask which of the two views is superior. In attacking Winch's 'relativism' by an appeal to science, Gellner therefore plays into Winch's hands. For, as Winch emphasises, there is no external criterion, be it scientific rationality or moral principle, in terms of which widely differing practices can be compared. He therefore denies that he is openly endorsing witchcraft and oracles, pointing out that it makes as little sense to justify them as it does to attack them. Evaluation of these practices does not lie within the province of the anthropologist or philosopher, who is concerned simply to understand the meaning of that practice within a particular form of life. Since the practitioners of witchcraft are not emulating Western science, no comparison of their results is necessary to see how they rate *vis-à-vis* Western science. Certainly, to dismiss these practices as superstition does not advance our understanding of that way of life.

But in denying the existence of an external criterion, Winch is not committed to a total relativism, according to which different cultures are incommensurable. In understanding alien societies we can take as a starting point the 'limiting notions' of birth, death and sex and consider the social institutions revolving around these activities.[23] The fact that rituals concerning birth, death and sex may be found in all forms of social life means that we are not insensitive to their meaning in primitive societies. Death, for example, is often accompanied by religious ideas and practices. But in determining what counts as a religious practice in an alien culture, we draw on our understanding of religion in our own society. While this constitutes a generalisation of our concept *of* religion, says Winch, it does not entail a generalisation *about* religion.[24] But even if we reject the view that science provides a superior evaluation of primitive culture, he argues, we can still draw on our own cultural experiences in understanding that society. Our cultural background embraces more than the language-game of science so the background against which we consider alien practices need not be a scientific one. If these objections to Wittgensteinian social philosophy can be overcome, then it would seem that the reconciliation between a Marxian and a Wittgensteinian approach assumes greater plausibility. This affinity becomes more intelligible if we consider the milieu within which Wittgenstein was writing.

Marx and Wittgenstein: common concerns

Evidence can be found of Wittgenstein's contact with Hegelian Marxism. To begin with, he had some knowledge of Hegelianism, albeit from a rather jaundiced standpoint, through his contact with Russell and his knowledge of Schopenhauer and Kierkegaard, Hegel's arch-critics. His representational theory of language advanced in the *Tractatus*, for example, had its origins in German rather than Anglo-Saxon philosophy, a point noted by Janik and Toulmin: 'By the time Wittgenstein came on the scene, this debate had been going on for some fifteen or twenty years in the drawing rooms of Vienna'.[25] Wittgenstein's later writings may also be traced to the problems facing European culture in the years leading up to the First World War.[26] Of greater interest is the influence of the economist Piero Sraffa, whom Wittgenstein acknowledged as the stimulus for the fundamental ideas of the *Investigations*.[27] Sraffa returned to the classical economics of Marx and Ricardo in developing a critique of marginalist economic theory.[28] His critique exhibits a basic similarity to the kinds of criticisms that Wittgenstein was to make of his earlier theory of language advanced in the *Tractatus*.

Marginalist theory is essentially formal and atomistic: it explores the relationship between economic man and the allocation of goods in isolation from the historical setting, overlooks the links between the factors of production and the class struggle and underestimates the significance of the level of the productive forces. Its basic assumption is that the market mechanism will ensure the most efficient allocation of scarce resources. Taking as its starting point the acceptance of a limited number of means geared to a multiplicity of competing ends, it formulates general laws, universally applicable and ultimately reducible to the central problem of the maximisation of utility. The theory is representational in so far as it sees its theoretical propositions as giving a correct description of the reality it pictures. It also sees itself as scientific in offering precise and general laws governing economic activity.

In *Production of Commodities by Means of Commodities*, Sraffa offers a new starting point for analysis, namely the reproducibility of commodities in capitalism instead of the needs of rational economic man.[29] Unlike the marginalists, who focus on the firms and the household, Sraffa acknowledges the significance of a wide range of factors, including the level of technology. He has therefore been seen as laying the foundations for a new paradigm.

The divergence between the two approaches is reflected in Wittgenstein's own development. In the *Tractatus* he advanced an atomistic conception of both theory and reality and a representational model of language, which assumed a correspondence between reality and language with objects corresponding directly to names in elementary propositions.[30] He claimed it was possible to construct a logical system of propositions, each describing a particular situation and giving a complete description of that part of the world which it makes sense to describe. His attempt to formulate a critique of language could be seen as analogous to the representational and universal theory of the marginalists. At the time, the atomism of the *Tractatus* was criticised by Bukharin who saw in it passivity, abstraction and distortion:

> The real subject, i.e. social and historical man ... does not in the least resemble that stenographer, inventing 'convenient' signs in shorthand, into whom the philosophising mathematicians and physicists desire to transform him (*B. Russell, Wittgenstein, Frank, Schlick*, and others). For he is actively transforming the world. He has changed the face of the whole of the earth ... We foretell objective changes in the world and we *change* the world. But this is unthinkable without real knowledge. Pure symbolism, stenography, a system of signs, of fictions, cannot serve as an instrument of *objective* changes, carried out by the subject.[31]

In the *Philosophical Investigations*, Wittgenstein came to share this view, rejecting the idea that the function of language was primarily to provide a description of the world, examining instead its use within a number of different kinds of activities or language-games. That Sraffa was largely responsible for this shift of direction was noted by Von Wright: 'it was above all Sraffa's acute and forceful criticism that compelled Wittgenstein to abandon his earlier views and to set out upon new roads. He said that his discussions with Sraffa made him feel like a tree from which all the branches had been cut'.[32] It was in the light of his discussions with Sraffa at Cambridge in the 1930s that Wittgenstein came to locate the meaning of words in their use rather than in their simple correspondence to reality, and abandoned the attempt to construct a general theory of language. In place of the representational theory of the *Tractatus*, according to which propositions derived their significance from a unified and formal structure, he adopted a more concrete approach in which the logic of language was seen as context-dependent:

> We see that what we call 'sentence' and 'language' has not the formal unity that I imagined, but is the family of structures more or less related to one another. – ... The question 'What is a word really?' is analogous to 'What is a piece in chess?'.[33]

His later theory of language even led to a revision of his concept of philosophical analysis: whereas his earlier work rested on an abstract distinction between simple and complex, in the later writings even this distinction was relativised and the very terms 'simple and complex' took their meaning from the context:

> But what are the simple constituent parts of which reality is composed? – What are the simple constituent parts of a chair ? – The bits of wood of which it is made? Or the molecules, or the atoms? – 'Simple' means: not composite. And here the point is: in what sense 'composite'? It makes no sense at all to speak absolutely of the 'simple parts of a chair'.[34]

There is a striking parallel between the Wittgensteinian emphasis upon the usage of words within a rule-governed context, rather than their underlying meanings, and the Marxian stress upon the use of commodities within a social context. This may be illustrated by Sraffa's account of the production of goods by means of goods but also by Marx's own argument in *Capital*, where he claims that the fetishistic nature of commodities can be demystified by a full understanding of their changing use and exchange-values.[35] 'Whether a use-value is to be regarded as raw material, as instrument of labour, or as product', says Marx, 'is determined entirely by its function in the labour-process, by the position it there occupies: as this varies, so does its character'.[36] He gives a number of examples to elucidate this point:

> Every object possesses various properties, and is thus capable of being applied to different uses. One and the same product may therefore serve as raw material in very different processes. Corn, for example, is a raw material for millers, starch-manufacturers, distillers and cattle-breeders. It also enters as raw material into

> its own production in the shape of seed; coal, too, is at the same time the product of, and a means of production in, coal-mining.
>
> Again a particular product may be used in one and the same process, both as an instrument of labour and as raw material. Take, for instance, the fattening of cattle, where the animal is the raw material, and at the same time an instrument for the production of manure.
>
> A product, though ready for immediate consumption, may yet serve as raw material for a further product, as grapes when they become the raw material for wine. On the other hand, labour may give us its product in such a form, that we can use it only as raw material, as is the case with cotton, thread and yarn. Such a raw material, though itself a product, may have to go through a whole series of different processes; in each of these in turn, it serves, with constantly varying form as raw material, until the last process of the series leaves it a perfect product, ready for individual consumption, or for use as an instrument of labour.[37]

The parallel here is, perhaps, not so surprising given the fundamental similarities in the views of language held by Marx and Wittgenstein. Both insist that language, as an expression of ideas, and social life are internally rather than contingently related. For Marx 'ideas do not exist separately from language'[38] and language, in turn, is portrayed as an integral feature of social life:

> Language is as old as consciousness, language *is* practical, real consciousness that exists for other men as well, and only therefore does it also exist for me; language, like consciousness, only arises from the need, the necessity, of intercourse with other men.[39]

For Wittgenstein, too, the study of language demanded an acceptance of its necessary relationship to social existence. For this reason he was scornful of attempts to construct new languages lacking a foundation in social intercourse:

> Esperanto. The feeling of disgust we get if we utter an *invented* word with invented derivative syllables. The word is cold, lacking in associations and yet it plays at being 'language'. A system of purely written signs would not disgust us so much.[40]

Thus, in using the tool-box metaphor (see Chapter V), Wittgenstein, like Marx, concentrates on what we *do* with language.[41] In this way, both seek to avoid the artificial distinction between ideas and the material world favoured by their contemporaries. Precisely because their contemporaries had accepted such a distinction, they were inevitably led into distortion. Marx therefore criticises speculative philosophy, as we saw earlier, for seeking to separate ideas from practical life, while Wittgenstein saw in metaphysics a tendency to arrest thought, to confine it within abstract determinations. Certain philosophical positions, he argued, inhibited people from seeing the obvious:

> People who are constantly asking 'why' are like tourists who stand in front of a building reading Baedeker and are so busy reading the history of its construction, etc., that they are prevented from *seeing* the building.[42]

But at the same time, both are ambivalent towards metaphysics. Marx's rejection of abstract speculation, as we saw earlier, did not prevent him from developing his own *philosophical* approach, which made full use of the principal categories of Hegelian metaphysics, including dialectic and alienation. Similarly, Wittgenstein's negative attitude towards metaphysics was matched by a considerable degree of respect. Denying that he was contemptuous of metaphysics, he describes 'the great metaphysical writings of the past as among the noblest productions of the human mind'.[43] Metaphysics, he argued, was part of the human condition, reflecting the desire to confront an ultimate reality which lies beyond the bounds of human discourse, and is an essential feature of the human striving for knowledge. But neither Marx nor Wittgenstein attempted a simple positivistic or common sense refutation of metaphysics but instead sought to discover its source. Marx therefore related abstract thought to particular stages of historical development rather than dismissing it as meaningless. Similarly, Wittgenstein was highly critical of attempts to refute metaphysics by an appeal to science or common sense. Instead, we should try to understand why we are led into metaphysical speculation:

> A philosopher is not a man out of his senses, a man who doesn't see what everybody sees; nor on the other hand is his disagreement with commonsense that of the scientist disagreeing with the coarse views of the man in the street. That is, his disagreement is not founded on a more subtle knowledge of fact. We therefore have to look round for the *source* of his puzzlement.[44]

Defending Heidegger when he was under attack from the Vienna circle, he said 'I can well understand what Heidegger means by *Sein* and *Angst*. Man has an impulse to run up against the boundaries of speech'.[45] For both Marx and Wittgenstein, metaphysical questions reflected basic human problems of a kind that could be transcended only by the elimination of the source of metaphysical speculation through the use of philosophical analysis. Their common commitment to an emancipatory conception of philosophy is expressed in Marx's description of philosophy as a major weapon of the working class and Wittgenstein's reference to using philosophy 'to shew the fly the way out of the fly-bottle'.[46] He makes the point more forcefully in *Culture and Value*:

> The solution of philosophical problems can be compared with a gift in a fairy tale: in the magic castle it appears enchanted and if you look at it outside in daylight it is nothing but an ordinary bit of iron (or something of the sort).[47]

But while Wittgenstein saw the development of therapeutic techniques as sufficient to secure freedom from metaphysical notions, for Marx, fundamental changes in the structure of social life were also necessary before the emancipation of the working class could be seen as complete.

The transcendence of the idealism–materialism distinction in Marxism and Wittgensteinian social philosophy is reflected in the rejection of an absolute distinction between causal and teleological explanations. Although it is often assumed that Marxism offers a teleological account of history, ascribing a meaning and goal to history, Marx in fact, following Hegel, fuses both kinds of explanations in his work. His account of ideology, for example, appears to constitute an external explanation since it refers to the objective characteristics of capitalist society, yet, at the same time, it presupposes that emancipation may be achieved through the self-reflection of the working class. Moreover, in Marx's account of the labour-process, mechanistic or causal principles are given an end, namely human praxis. Teleology enters into mechanism for Marx when he attributes ends to history and classes: by working with machines and tools, men are able to use their knowledge of the laws of nature as a means of satisfying their needs and desires. He deals with this point at length in his essay on the labour-process in *Capital*, where he draws heavily on Hegel's *Science of Logic*, thereby providing further evidence of his long-standing commitment to Hegelianism:

> Labour is, in the first place, a process in which both Man and Nature participate, and in which man of his own accord starts, regulates, and controls the material re-actions between himself and Nature. He opposes himself to Nature as one of her own forces, setting in motion arms and legs, head and hands, the natural forces of his body, in order to appropriate Nature's productions in a form adapted to his own wants. By thus acting on the external world and changing it, he at the same time changes his own nature.[48]

The labour-process for Marx is not merely a mechanical process but one in which men creatively bring about a change in the material world through their actions. It is in this context that he introduces his well-known example of the bee and the architect, elucidating his notion of species-being explored in the 'Economic and philosophical manuscripts'.[49] For Marx, the work of the worst architect is superior to that of the bee in so far as the architect has a conception of what he is seeking to construct and is able to bring it into being through his efforts:

> In the labour-process, therefore, man's activity with the help of the instruments of labour, effects an alteration designed from the commencement, in the material worked upon ... Nature's material adapted by a change of form in the wants of man.

> Labour has incorporated itself with its subject: the former is materialised, the latter transformed.[50]

> At the end of every labour-process we get a result that already existed in the imagination of the labourer at its commencement. He not only effects a change of form in the material on which he works, but he also realises a purpose of his own that gives the law to his *modus operandi.*[51]

In work, teleology and causality are mutually interdependent for man harnesses nature's laws, employing nature against herself as a means of achieving his specific human ends:

> He makes use of the mechanical, physical and chemical properties of some substances in order to make other substances subservient to his aims. Leaving out of consideration such ready-made means of subsistence as fruits, in gathering which a man's own limbs serve as the instruments of his labour, the first thing of which the labourer possesses himself is not the subject of labour but its instrument. Thus nature becomes one of the organs of his activity, one that he annexes to his own bodily organs, adding stature to himself in spite of the Bible. As the earth is his original larder, so too it is his original tool house. It supplies him, for instance, with stones for throwing, grinding, pressing, cutting, &c. The earth itself is an instrument of labour, but when used as such in agriculture implies a whole series of other instruments and a comparatively high development of labour. No sooner does labour undergo the least development than it requires specially prepared instruments ... The use and fabrication of instruments of labour, although existing in the germ among certain species of animals, is specifically characteristic of the human labour-process, and Franklin therefore defines man as a tool-making animal.[52]

In Wittgensteinian social philosophy we find a rejection of both poles of the teleology–causality dichotomy in Winch's recommendations regarding the appropriate methods for the social sciences.[53] On the one hand, Winch rejects causal explanations in favour of explanations in terms of reasons and purposes, on the grounds that the differences in subject-matter between the social and natural sciences demand very different models of explanation. Given that social action embodies a subjective element lacking in the natural world, it follows, for Winch, that statistical laws and causal generalisations can have no part to play in our understanding of social life. But at the same time he denies, as we saw earlier, that an exclusion of causal explanation rules out the possibility of constraint. On the other hand, while favouring explanations in terms of reasons and motives, Winch argues that these in turn can only be understood by relating them to the context in which the action takes place. He therefore invokes Wittgenstein's notion of grammar in setting out his *idea* of a social science: understanding an action, for Winch, means grasping the grammatical rules which are being followed rather than studying the purposes of the individual agent. By focusing on shared rules rather than private experiences, he rules out any appeal to empathy or intuition. We do not need to relive the experiences of others in our minds, he argues, attacking the familiar Wittgensteinian target, the argument from analogy, but rather to understand the rule which is being followed by relating the action to the context in which it occurs. Like Marx, Winch appeals to the practice of everyday life in challenging a traditional philosophical dichotomy.

While a number of basic similarities between Marxism and Wittgensteinian social philosophy may be discerned in their theories of language, approach to metaphysics and conception of the methods of the social sciences, nonetheless we find a fundamental difference on the question of political commitment. Wittgenstein's political stance, unlike that of Marx's, was decidedly ambiguous. His work was coloured by his inability or disinclination to draw links between language and class, thereby encouraging accusations of conservatism. While in his major philosophical works, including the *Remarks on the Foundations of Mathematics, The Blue and Brown Books, Philosophical Investigations* and *On Certainty*, Wittgenstein offers an approach to philosophical problems resembling that of Hegelian Marxism, for example, in its conceptions of philosophy, its understanding of the nature of social change, the relationship between facts and values, and the notion of a world-view, whenever Wittgenstein wrote explicitly on social or political issues, his conclusions differed radically from those of Marx. While Marx endorses working-class struggles, Wittgenstein's thoughts on this subject in a recently published work reveal a narrowly minded, moralistic and unreflecting attitude: 'I believe that bad housekeeping within the state fosters bad housekeeping in families. A workman who is constantly ready to go on strike will not bring up his children to respect order either'.[54] Indeed, Pascal has observed that 'at a time when intellectual Cambridge was turning Left, he was still an old-time conservative of the late Austro-Hungarian empire'.[55] What is odd is that Wittgenstein's obvious interest in the sociology of knowledge, expressed in his analysis of forms of life, should have failed to extend to an historical approach. In this sense he was 'out of key' with the mood of his time, differing from many of his contemporaries who, during the inter-war years, saw the opportunity for bringing about social change. But Wittgenstein 'wanted none of this historicism. To him, historical variety and change possessed no more philosophical relevance than they had done for Plato, Descartes, or for his much-admired Frege. In one of the surviving pre-*Tractatus* notebooks, we find him jotting down the curious remark, "What is history to me? Mine is the first and only world"'.[56] Wittgenstein cut himself adrift from the movement for reconstruction, retaining an individualistic apolitical stance which reflected the disillusionment characteristic of intellectual life in the *pre*-war period. Keynes, for example, writing in the early 1920s, saw Wittgenstein as epitomising the alienation of intellectuals.

> ... Every one of our religious and political constructions is moth-eaten ... Our official religions have about as much practical influence on us as the monarchy or the Lord Mayor's coach. But we no longer substitute for them the militant scepticism of Voltaire and Hume, or the humanitarian optimism of Bentham and Comte and Mill, or the far-fetched abstractions of Hegel. Our newest Spinoza (Wittgenstein) gives us frozen comfort.[57]

In this context he refers to Wittgenstein's remark in the *Tractatus* that 'We feel that even when *all possible* scientific questions have been answered, the problems of life remain completely untouched. Of course there are then no questions left, and this itself is the answer'.[58]

On the other hand, Wittgenstein's apoliticism and ahistoricism can be exaggerated. Although he remained wedded to a Tolstoyan individualism throughout his life, he could not have been oblivious to the political events of his time. His immediate circle included men such as Sraffa, working out the framework for a new analysis of capitalism, a Russian exile, Nicholas Bachtin, described as a 'fiery communist' and a close friend, mathematician Francis Skinner who volunteered to fight with the International Brigade in Spain. Pascal has drawn attention to Wittgenstein's concern over unemployment and the outbreak of war, 'But he would not', she says, 'react to their impact as others might. He would not quote things said by Lenin and Stalin, and it is inane to affix any political label to him'.[59] Moran has also drawn attention to Wittgenstein's anti-political rather than apolitical stance.[60] While Wittgenstein seems to have been sympathetic to the aims of Marxism he found practical politics distasteful. When reading *Capital*, moreover, Wittgenstein seems to have objected to Marx's *style* of writing.[61] As is well known, Wittgenstein took great interest in the Soviet Union. At one stage he hoped to settle there, and visited Russia twice; in 1935, with the help of Keynes, when he was offered, but declined, the chair of philosophy at Kazan, and again in 1939. However, it is debatable how far Wittgenstein's desire to settle in Russia stemmed from an ideological commitment or from his sympathy to the Russian way of life acquired from his reading of Tolstoy. Wittgenstein's attitude to Russia reflects the degree to which the emphasis on the 'personal' in his pre-war and inter-war writings continued to persist uneasily in the culturalism of the later works, influenced by Sraffa.

But given the apparent ahistoricism of the work of Wittgenstein and his followers, can the claim for an affinity between Marx and Wittgenstein be upheld? The major justification for drawing Marx and Wittgenstein more closely together lies in Wittgenstein's constant efforts to provide a critique of linguistic alienation, which he saw as a central problem of philosophy:

> We are struggling with language.
> We are engaged in a struggle with language.[62]

> One keeps forgetting to go right down to the foundations. One doesn't put the question marks *deep* enough down.[63]

While Marx provided a broad historical framework within which to examine alienation, Wittgenstein, accepting that language goes 'on holiday', examined specific forms of linguistic alienation but abstracted his language-games from social and historical circumstances. He failed to examine fully the origins of philosophical puzzles in social and historical life, although he accepted that this was where their origins must lie. Whilst Wittgenstein was very much concerned with the *phenomenon* of linguistic alienation, he never sought to relate it to other forms of alienation but saw it as a problem facing the individual, describing the philosopher as 'a man who has to cure many intellectual diseases in himself before he can arrive at the notions of common sense'.[64] Lacking a social theory to give an impetus to his primarily philosophical investigations, his examination ground to a halt at the nature of language, instead of progressing to a study of the specific historical conditions underpinning this alienation of the kind found in Marxism. This is not to detract from his contribution, since any study of alienation is furthered by the study of the mechanics of linguistic alienation, but the underlying social causes of alienation have to be examined. It might be argued that Wittgenstein had no need to delve into social and political affairs since he was concerned with philosophical problems. But, as I have tried to show, even on Wittgenstein's own terms philosophy and practice cannot be separated so to excuse Wittgenstein's neglect of social questions on the grounds that he was a philosopher is unsatisfactory, particularly in view of the fact that he was himself reacting against the separation of philosophy from ordinary language and ordinary life. Like Marx, he seeks to answer to philosophical problems in everyday life but he does not penetrate quite so deeply as Marx. Yet he was not without hope that his philosophical approach would generate a new way of thinking: 'A present-day teacher of philosophy doesn't select food for his pupil with the aim of flattering his taste, but with the aim of changing it'.[65] But at the same time he was conscious of the limitations of philosophy in both understanding and changing the world. For this reason he advised his students to eschew professional philosophy in favour of either honest manual labour or medicine, although this reveals the influence of Tolstoy rather than Marx. His own dissatisfaction with the academic philosophy of his time seems to be a direct result of his estimation of the superficiality of philosophical analysis. However, as we have seen, his dissatisfaction culminated in a moral rather than a philosophical solution. Despite the difficulties encountered in reconciling Wittgenstein and Marx, the evidence suggests that Wittgenstein's work is of value in casting fresh light on problems raised within humanist Marxism and in the social sciences in general.[66] That such a reconciliation is possible establishes Wittgenstein as a progressive philosopher and demonstrates the strength of the philosophical basis of humanist Marxism.

Notes to Chapter VIII

[1] P. Winch, *The Idea of a Social Science*; 'Understanding a primitive society'.

[2] T. Benton, 'Winch, Wittgenstein and Marxism', *Radical Philosophy* XIII (spring 1976), pp. 1–6; K. T. Fann, 'Wittgenstein and bourgeois philosophy', *Radical Philosophy* VIII (summer 1964); A. R. Manser, *The End of Philosophy: Marx and Wittgenstein* (Inaugural address, the University of Southampton, 1973).

[3] Benton, *op. cit*.

[4] It should be borne in mind that Winch has (slightly) modified his position since the initial publication of *The Idea of a Social Science* but his overall framework of social explanation remains unchanged. (See, for example, P. Winch, 'Language, belief and relativism', *Contemporary British Philosophy*.) But even within this framework, Winch claims to resolve many of the problems raised by his critics.

[5] A. MacIntyre, 'The idea of a social science', *The Philosophy of Social Explanation*, ed. A. Ryan (Oxford: University Press, 1973), p. 16.

[6] K. Marx, 'Preface to contribution to critique of political economy', *Selected Writings in Sociology and Social Philosophy* ed. by Bottomore and Rubel (London: Pelican, 1963), p. 68.

[7] P. Winch, unpublished, *Notes to Joint Session* (Swansea, 1967). This paper constitutes a reply to MacIntyre, *op. cit*.

[8] S. Henry, 'It fell off the back of a lorry', *New Society* (26 Feb., 1976), pp. 427–9.

[9] P. Winch, *Notes to Joint Session*.

[10] A. MacIntyre, *op. cit*.

[11] E. Goffman, *Asylums* (London: Pelican, 1968).

[12] P. Winch, *Notes to Joint Session*.

[13] Gellner, for example, makes much of what he sees as Winch's acceptance of primitive practices; E. Gellner, 'The new idealism – cause and meaning in the social sciences', *Positivism and Sociology*, ed. A. Giddens (London: Heinemann, 1974), pp. 129–56.

[14] K. Marx and F. Engels, 'Manifesto of the Communist Party'.

[15] Winch, 'Language, belief and relativism'; Marx, 'Contribution to the critique of Hegel's philosophy of law'.

[16] L. Wittgenstein, 'Remarks on Frazer's *Golden Bough*', *Wittgenstein: Sources and Perspectives*, ed. C. G. Luckhardt, (Hassocks: Harvester Press, 1979), pp. 61–2.

[17] *Ibid.*, p. 63.

[18] *Ibid.*, pp. 68–9.

[19] However, Winch does tend to draw too radical a distinction between science and religion in this respect. In many cases, the situation in science is equally confused, with theories being rejected or accepted on apparently arbitrary grounds; see, for example, T. S. Kuhn, *The Structure of Scientific Revolutions*; P. K. Feyerabend, *Against Method* and *Science in a Free Society* (London: New Left Books, 1978); F. Capra, *The Tao of Physics* (London: Fontana, 1976).

[20] P. Winch, 'Understanding a primitive society'.

[21] Gellner, *op. cit.*, pp. 151–2.

[22] Habermas, *Towards a Rational Society*; H. Marcuse, *One-Dimensional Man* (London: Routledge and Kegan Paul, 1964).

[23] P. Winch, 'Understanding a primitive society'.

[24] P. Winch, *Notes to Joint Session.*

[25] A. Janik and S. Toulmin, *Wittgenstein's Vienna*, p. 31.

[26] As Janik and Toulmin point out, 'At the time Wittgenstein appeared to be spinning the whole substance of his later philosophy out of his head, like some intellectually creative spider; in fact, much of his material had origins that his English audiences knew next to nothing about, and many of the problems he chose to concentrate on had been under discussion among German-speaking philosophers and psychologists since before the First World War' (*op. cit.*, p. 22).

[27] See L. Wittgenstein, *Philosophical Investigations*, p. iii.

[28] P. Sraffa, *Production of Commodities by Means of Commodities* (Cambridge: University Press, 1960). While it has been argued that Sraffa takes as given the existence of capitalism without exploring its origins and development, Roncaglio claims that Sraffa has made a decisive contribution to Marxist economics, firstly by showing how labour-values are related to the determination of prices of production but also by offering a critique of marginalist theory, which was itself designed to refute Marxism. A. Roncaglio, *Sraffa and the Theory of Prices* (Chichester: John Wiley, 1978).

[29] P. Sraffa, *op. cit.*

[30] As Wittgenstein says in the *Tractatus*: 'The world is the totality of facts, not of things' (1. 1); 'The totality of true thoughts is a picture of the world' (3. 01); 'In a proposition a thought can be expressed in such a way that elements of the propositional sign correspond to the objects of the thought' (3. 2).

[31] N. Bukharin, 'Theory and practice from the standpoint of dialectical materialism', pp. 17–18.

[32] G. H. Von Wright, 'Biographical sketch', included in N. Malcolm, *Ludwig Wittgenstein: A Memoir* (Oxford: University Press, 1966), p. 15.

[33] L. Wittgenstein, *Philosophical Investigations*, 108.

[34] *Ibid.*, 47.

[35] P. Sraffa, *op. cit.*; K. Marx, *Capital.*

[36] K. Marx, *Capital* I, p. 182.

[37] *Ibid.*, p. 182.

[38] K. Marx, *Grundrisse*, p. 163.

[39] K. Marx and F. Engels, 'The German ideology', *Collected Works* V, p. 44.

[40] L. Wittgenstein, *Culture and Value*, p. 52e.

[41] See L. Wittgenstein, *Philosophical Investigations*, 11.

[42] L. Wittgenstein, *Culture and Value*, p. 40e.

[43] L. Wittgenstein, quoted in K. T. Fann, *Wittgenstein's Conception of Philosophy* (Oxford: Basil Blackwell, 1969) p. 86.

[44] L. Wittgenstein, *The Blue and Brown Books* (Oxford: Basil Blackwell, 1969), p. 59.

[45] L. Wittgenstein, quoted in S. Toulmin, 'Wittgenstein', *Encounter* XXXII, 1 (Jan. 1969), p. 63.

[46] K. Marx, 'Contribution to critique of Hegel's philosophy of law. Introduction', *Collected Works* III; L. Wittgenstein, *Philosophical Investigations*, 309.

[47] L. Wittgenstein, *Culture and Value*, p. 11e.

[48] K. Marx, *Capital* I, p. 177.

[49] *Ibid.*, p. 178.

[50] *Ibid.*, p. 180.

[51] *Ibid.*, p. 178.

[52] *Ibid.*, p. 179.

[53] P. Winch, *The Idea of a Social Science and its Relation to Philosophy*.

[54] L. Wittgenstein, *Culture and Value*, p. 63e.

[55] F. Pascal, 'Wittgenstein: a personal memoir', *Wittgenstein: Sources and Perspectives*, ed. C. G. Luckhardt (Hassocks: Harvester Press, 1979), p. 28.

[56] A. Janik and S. Toulmin, *Wittgenstein's Vienna*, p. 243.

[57] J. M. Keynes, 'Reconstruction in Europe', *The Collected Writings of John Maynard Keynes*, XVII (Cambridge: University Press, 1977), p. 449.

[58] L. Wittgenstein, *Tractatus Logico-Philosophicus*, 6. 52.

[59] F. Pascal, *op. cit.*, pp. 54–5.

[60] J. Moran, 'Wittgenstein and Russia', *New Left Review* (1972), pp. 85–96.

[61] *Ibid.*

[62] L. Wittgenstein, *Culture and Value*, p. 11e.

[63] *Ibid.*, p. 62e.

[64] *Ibid.*, p. 44e.

[65] *Ibid.*, p. 17e.

[66] See for example, R. Beardsmore, *Art and Morality*; D. Z. Phillips, *The Concept of Prayer* (London: Routledge and Kegan Paul, 1965), *Religion and Understanding* (Oxford: Basil Blackwell, 1967); J. W. Danford, *Wittgenstein and Political Philosophy* (Chicago: University Press, 1978); H. Pitkin, *Wittgenstein and Justice* (Berkeley, Cal.: University of California Press, 1972).

Index

Name index

Subject index